Theo von Taane

FUNCRAFT
DAS INOFFIZIELLE
NOTIZBUCH
FÜR MINECRAFT FANS

(Auch geeignet als Spielebogenpapier für das Buch „FUNCRAFT Offline Buchspiele")

KEIN OFFIZIELLES MINECRAFT-PRODUKT. NICHT VON MOJANG GENEHMIGT ODER MIT MOJANG VERBUNDEN.

Bibliografische Information der Deutschen Nationalbibliothek: Die Deutsche Nationalbibliothek verzeichnet diese Publikation in der Deutschen Nationalbibliografie; detaillierte bibliografische Daten sind im Internet über http://dnb.dnb.de abrufbar.

© 2017 Theo von Taane; 3. Auflage
Covergrafik & Illustrationen © Theo von Taane

Herstellung und Verlag: BoD – Books on Demand, Norderstedt

ISBN: 9783743196889

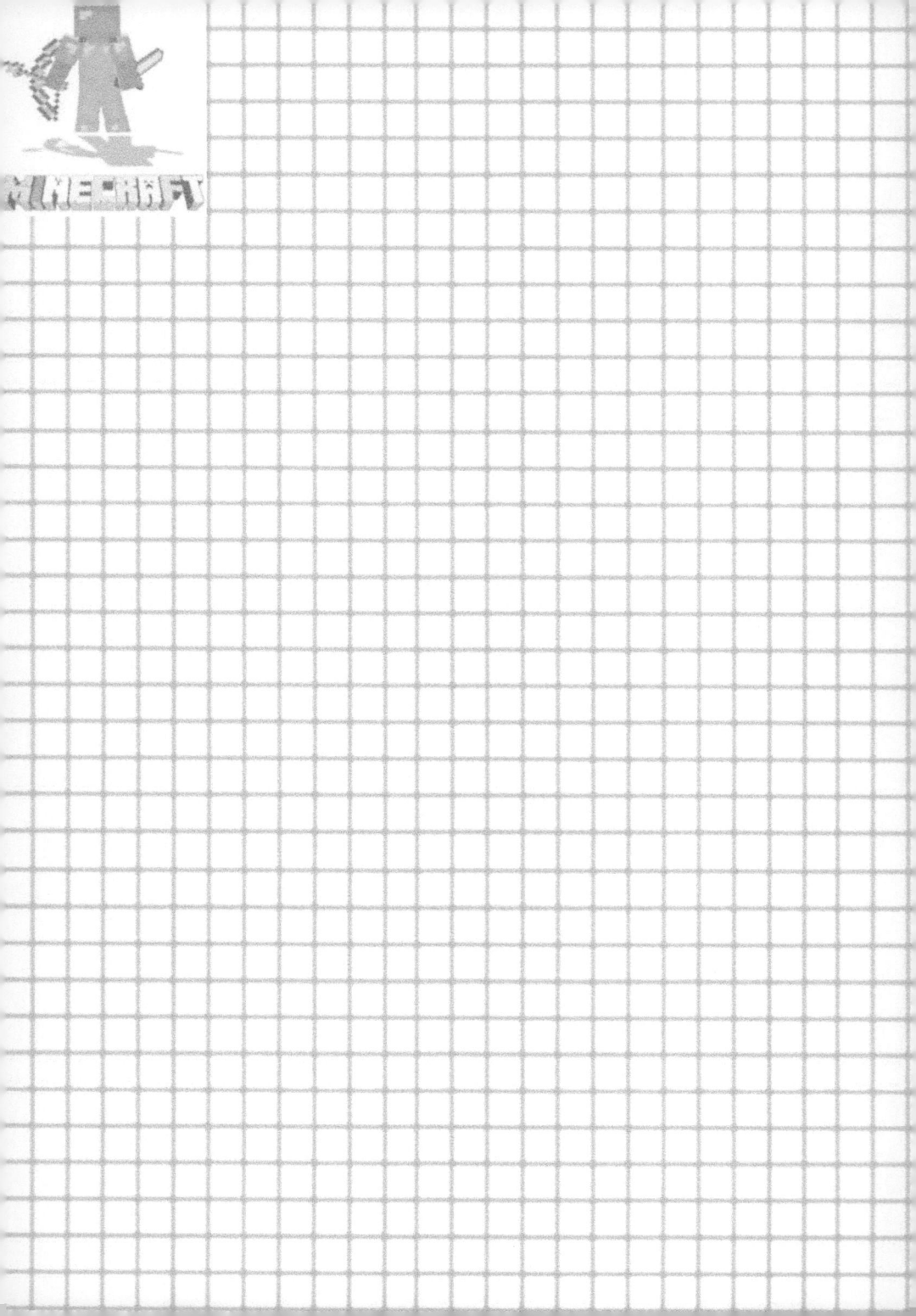

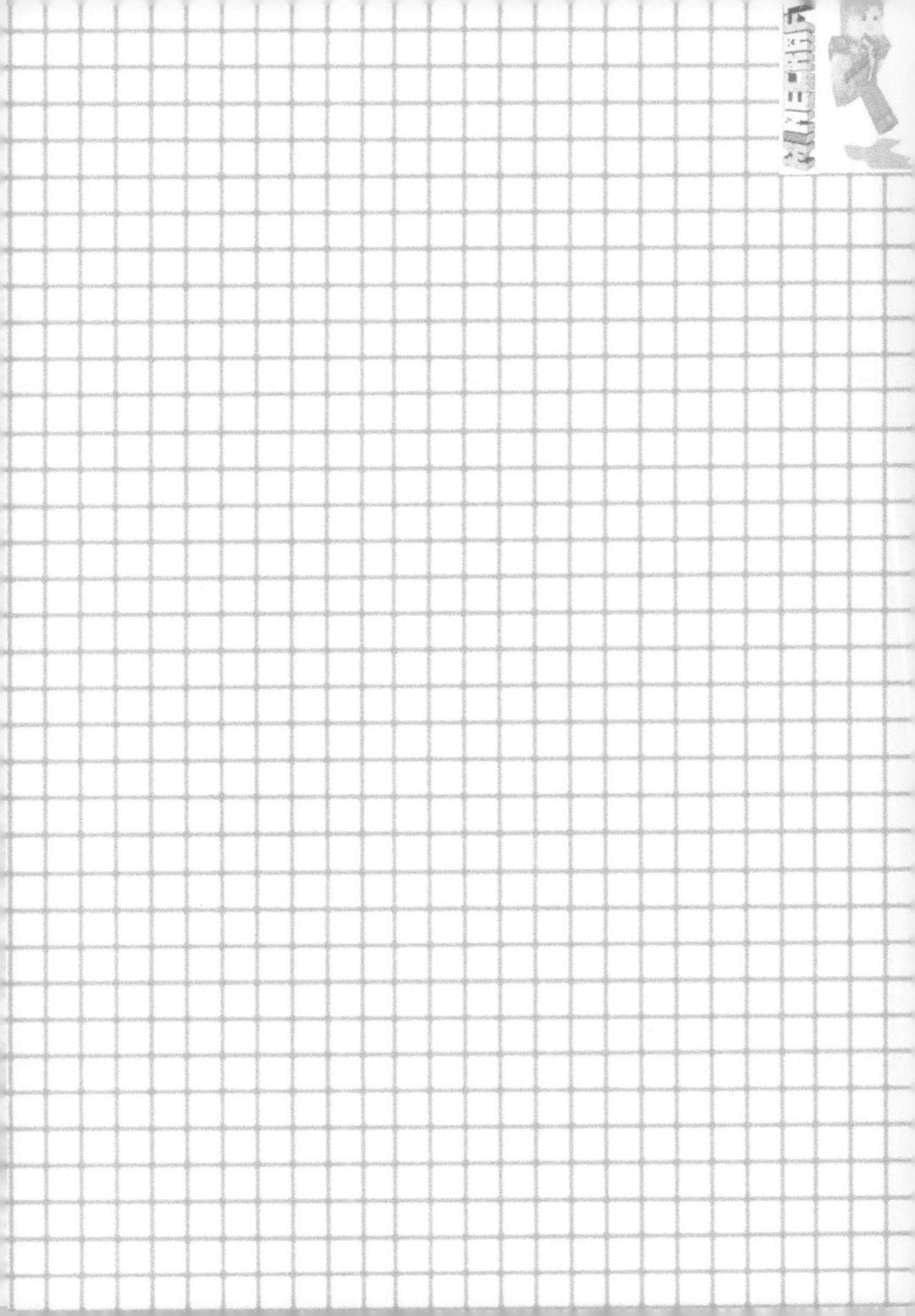

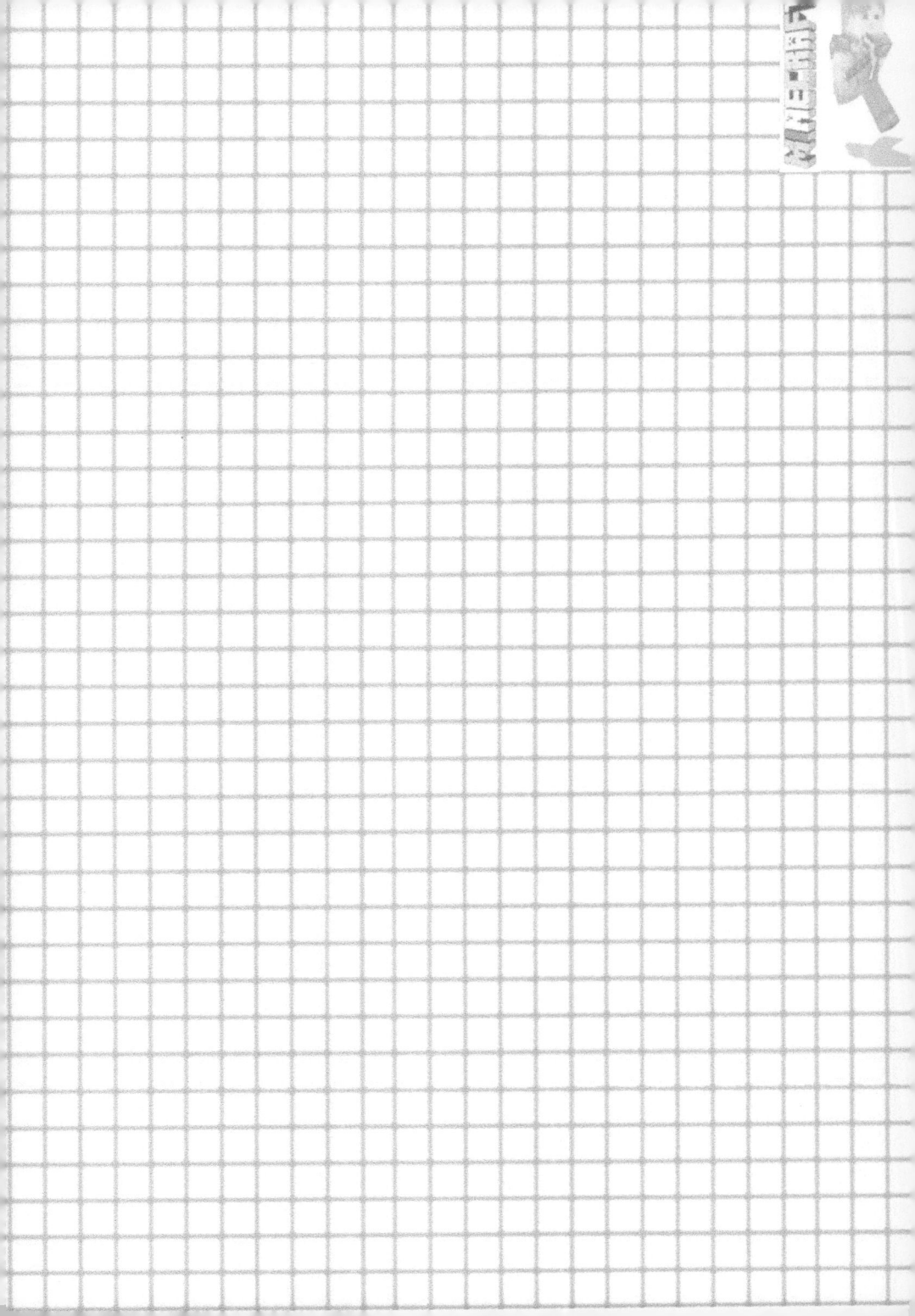

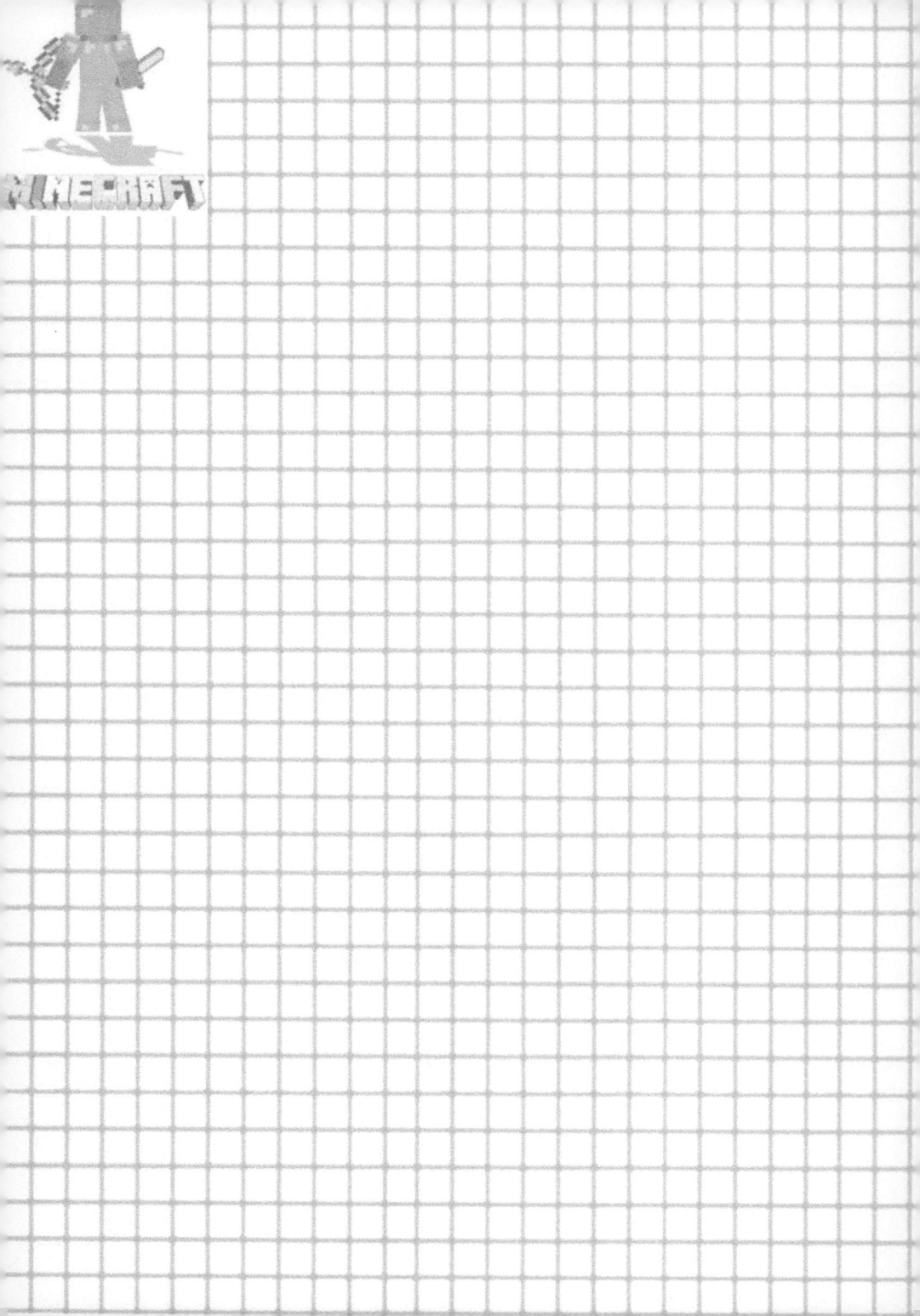

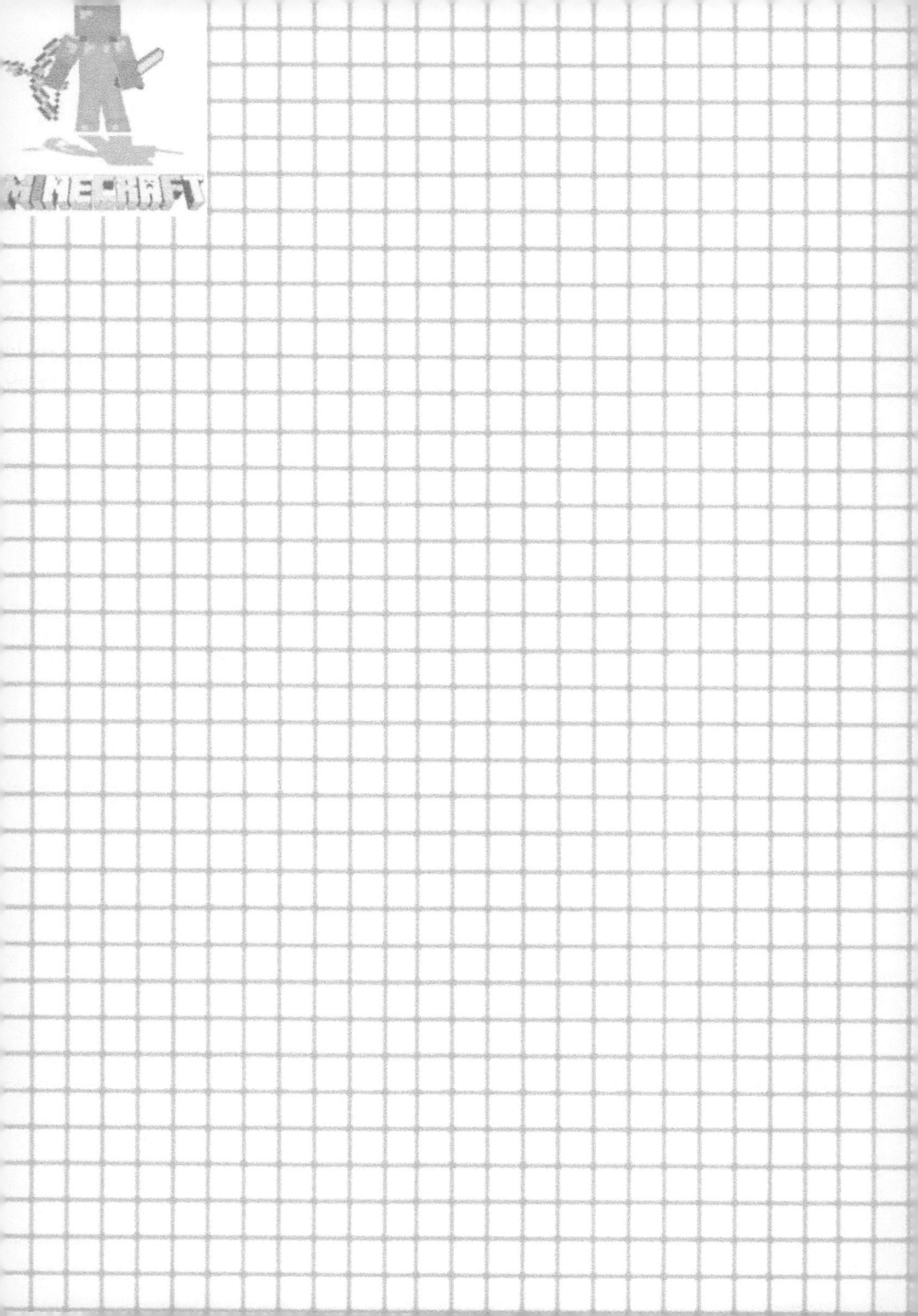

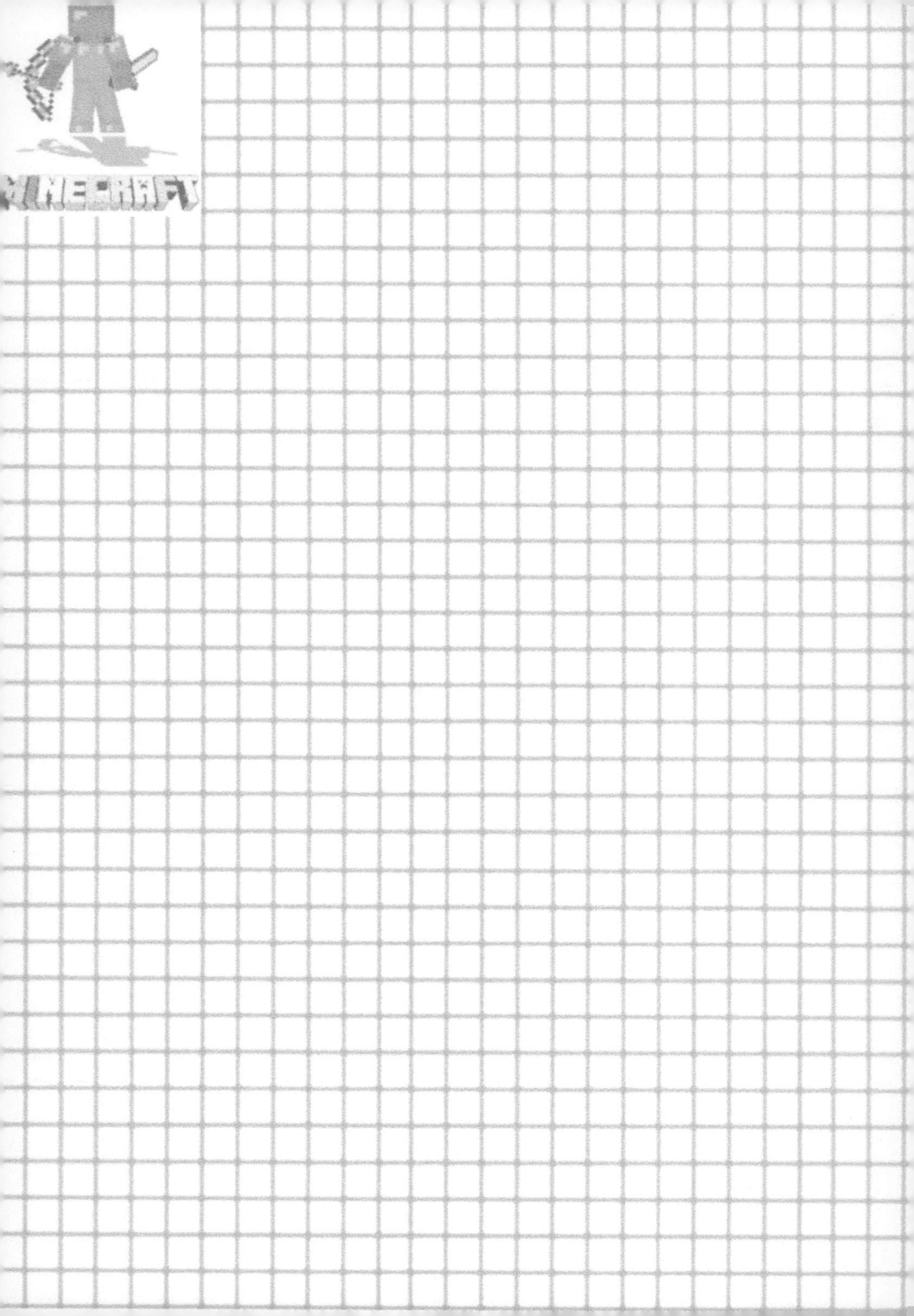

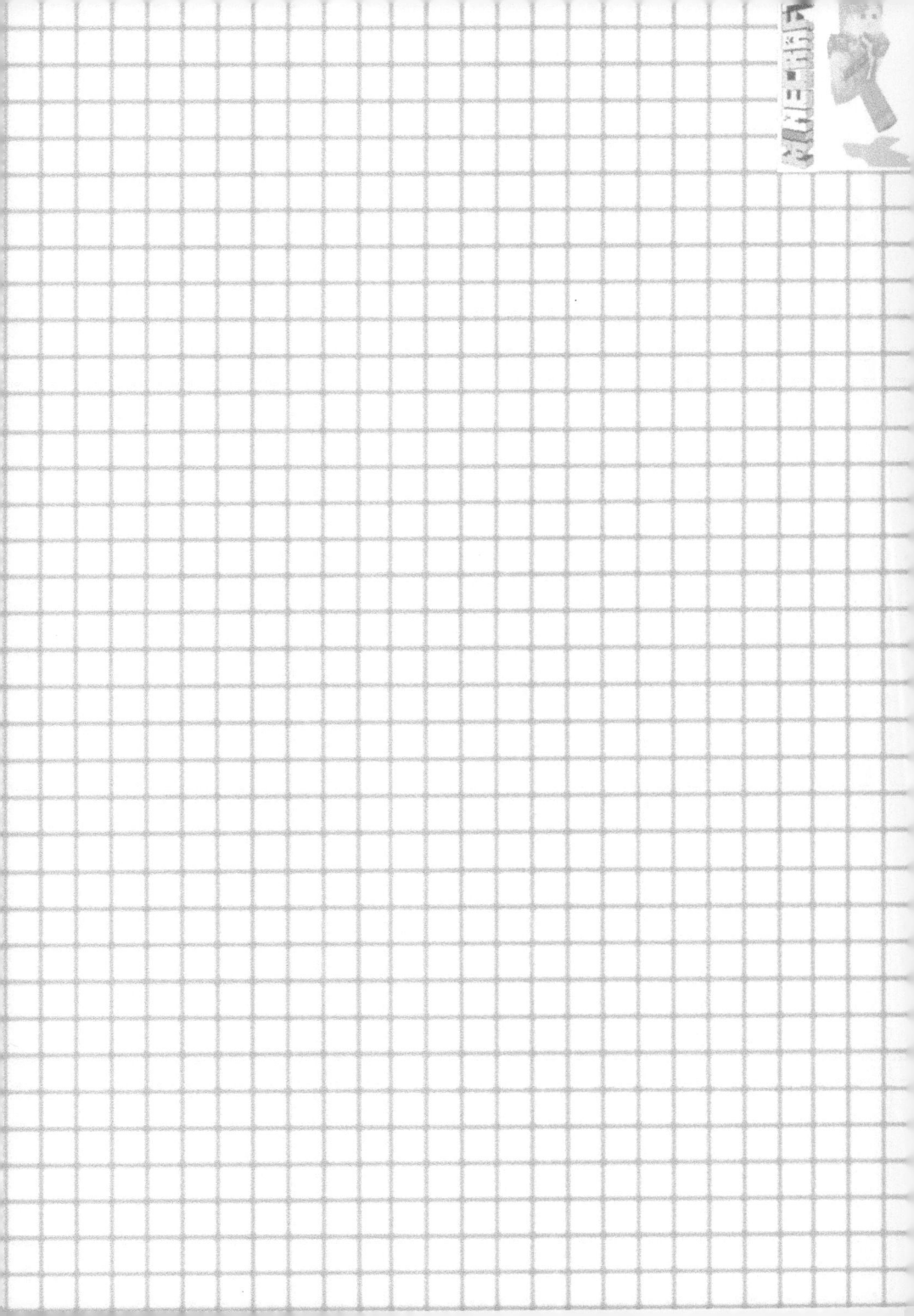

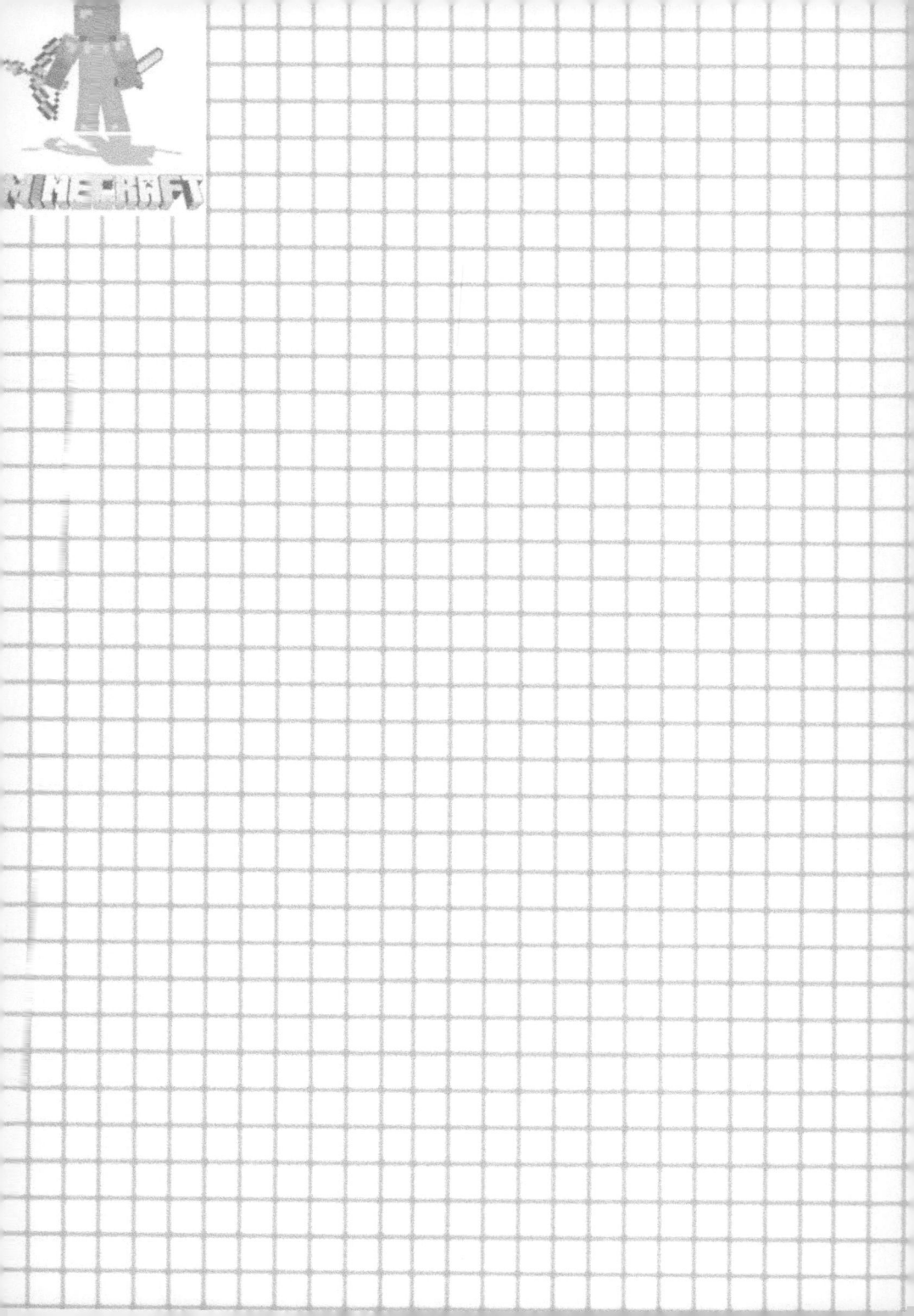

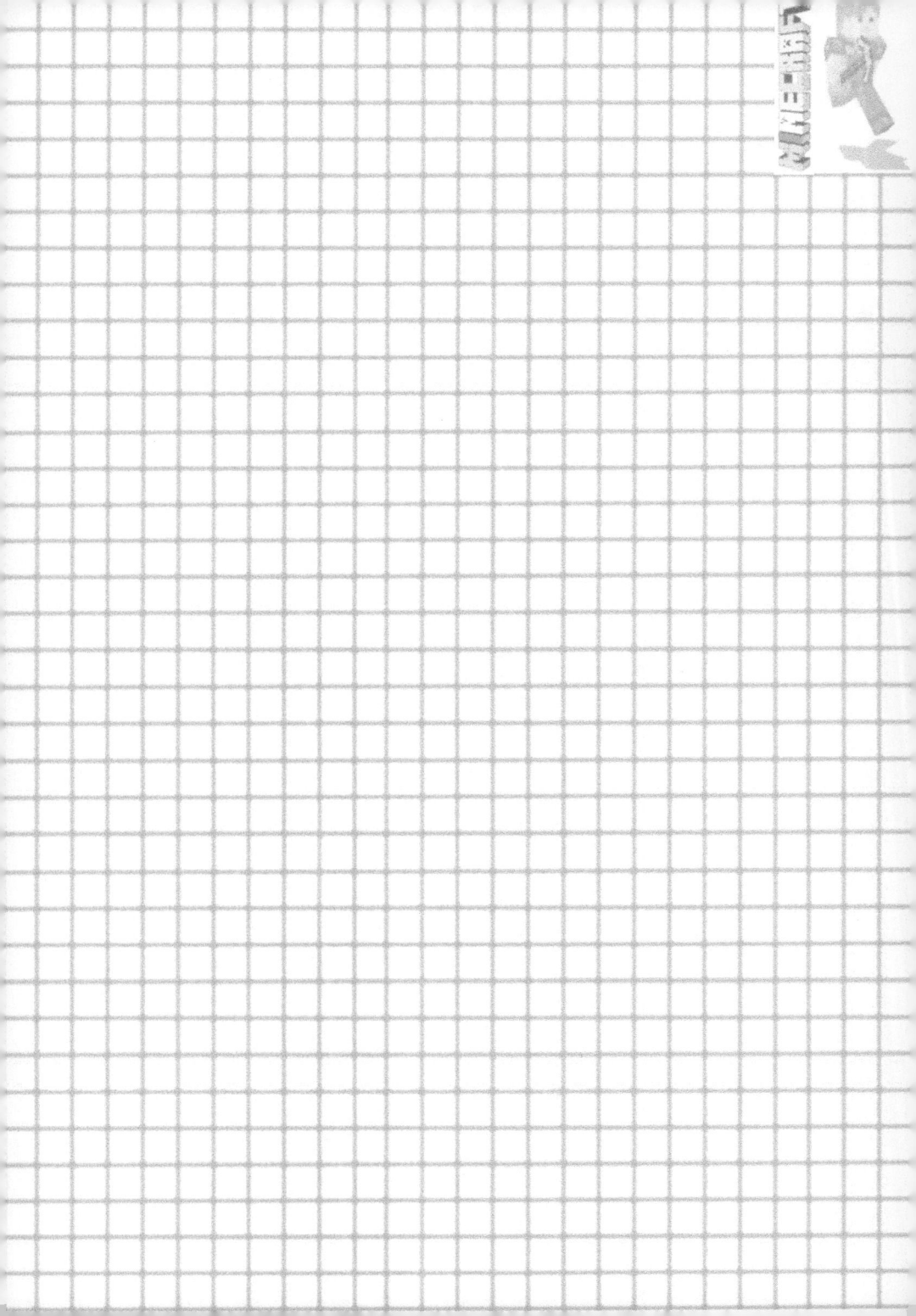

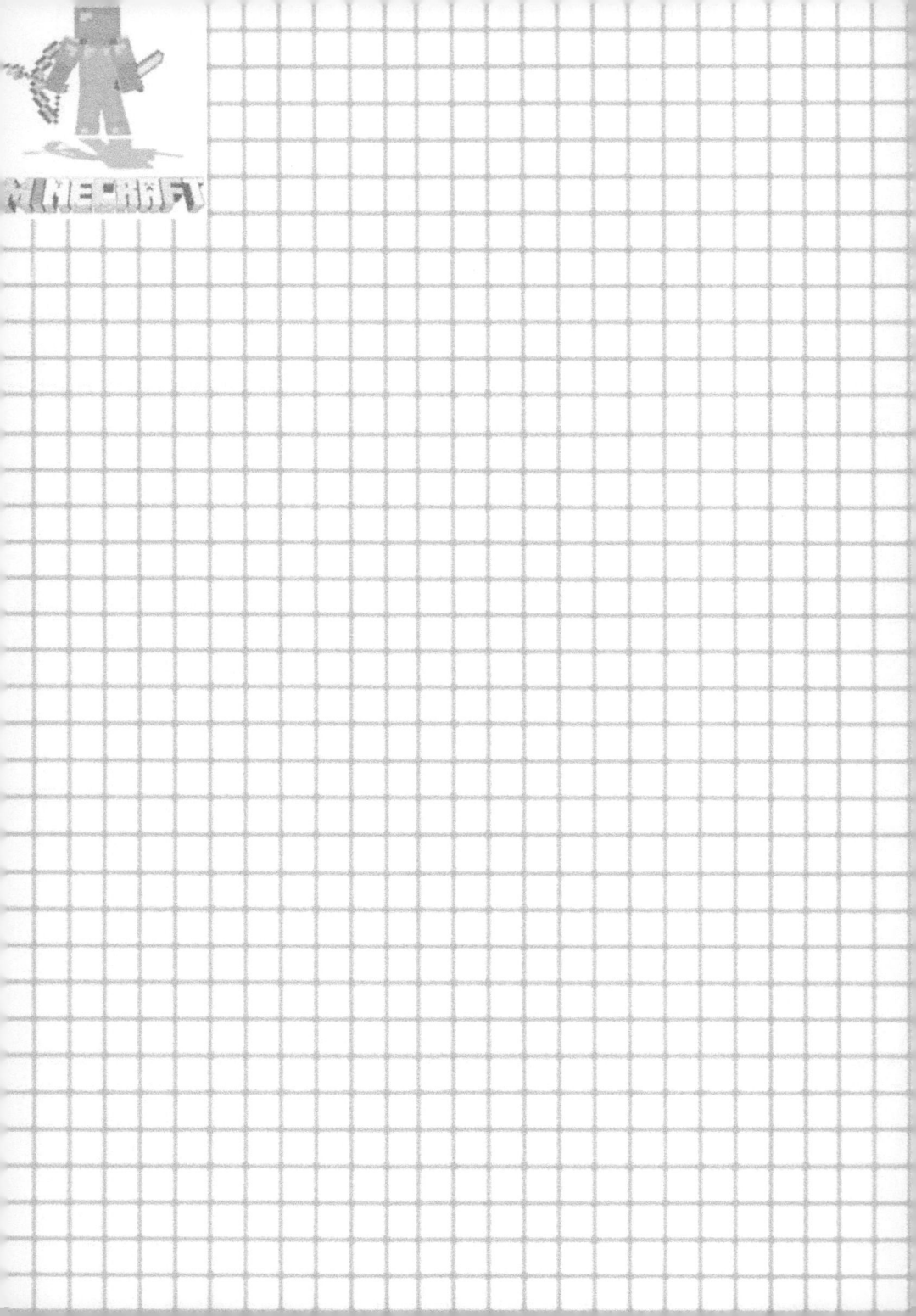

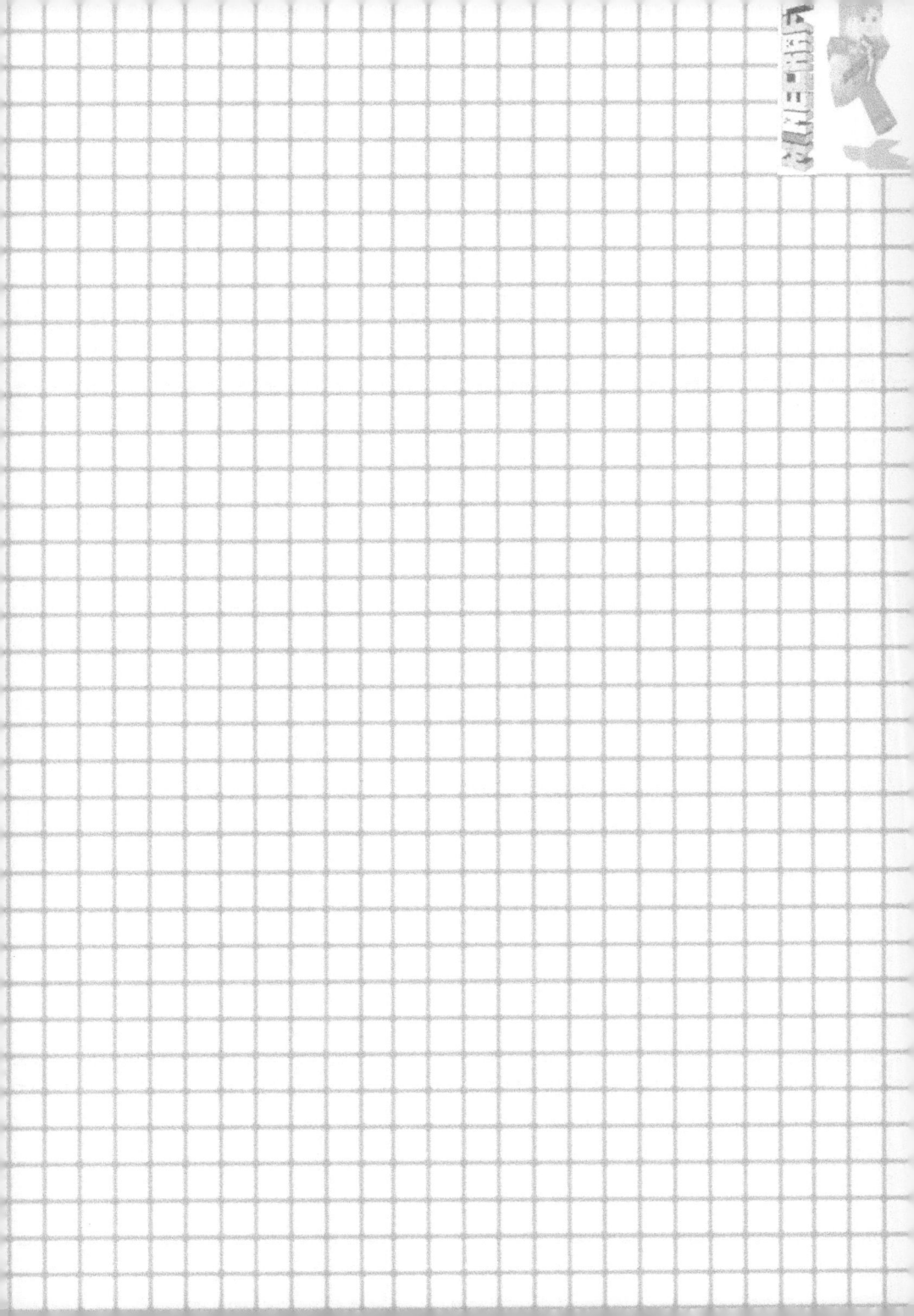

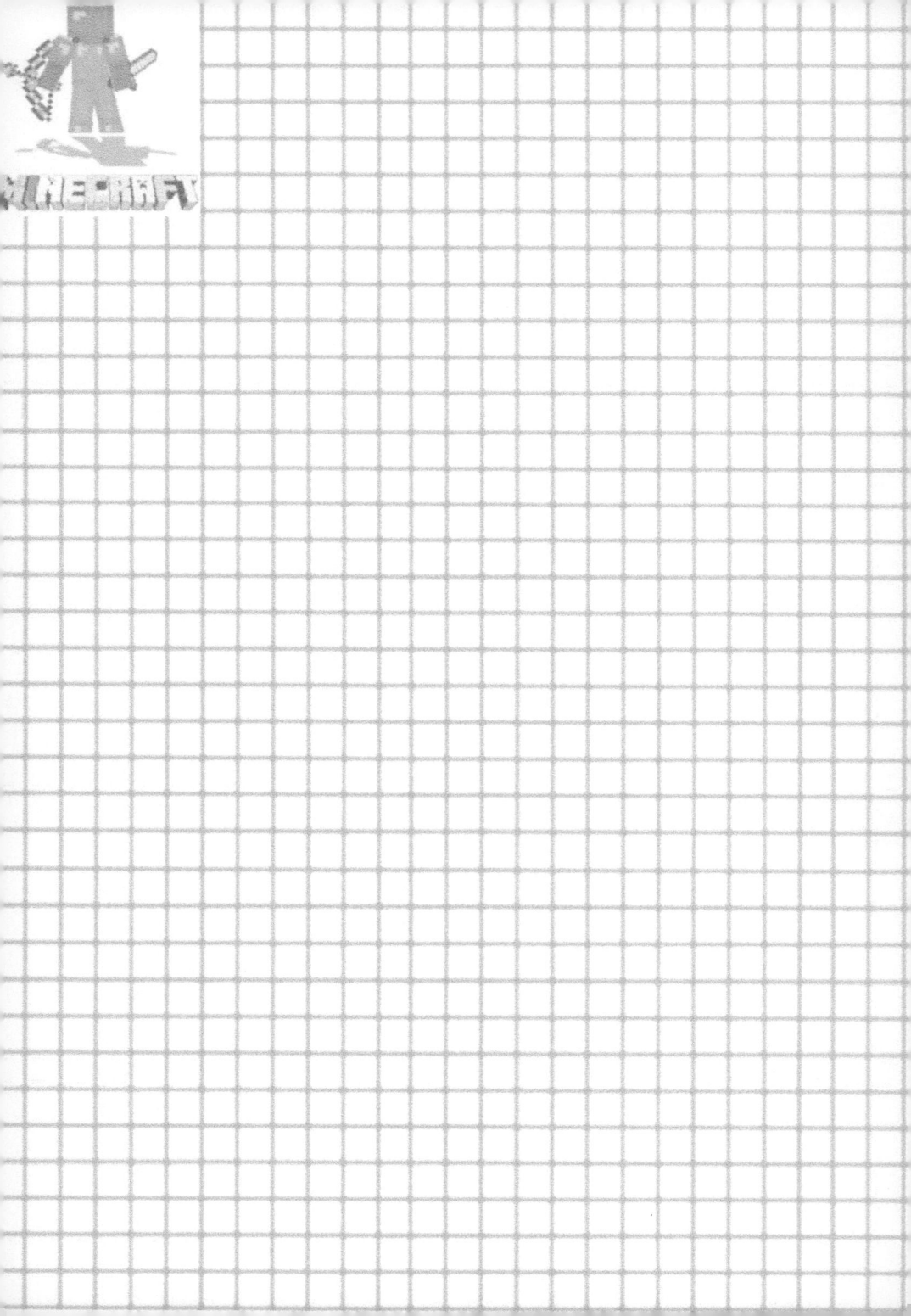

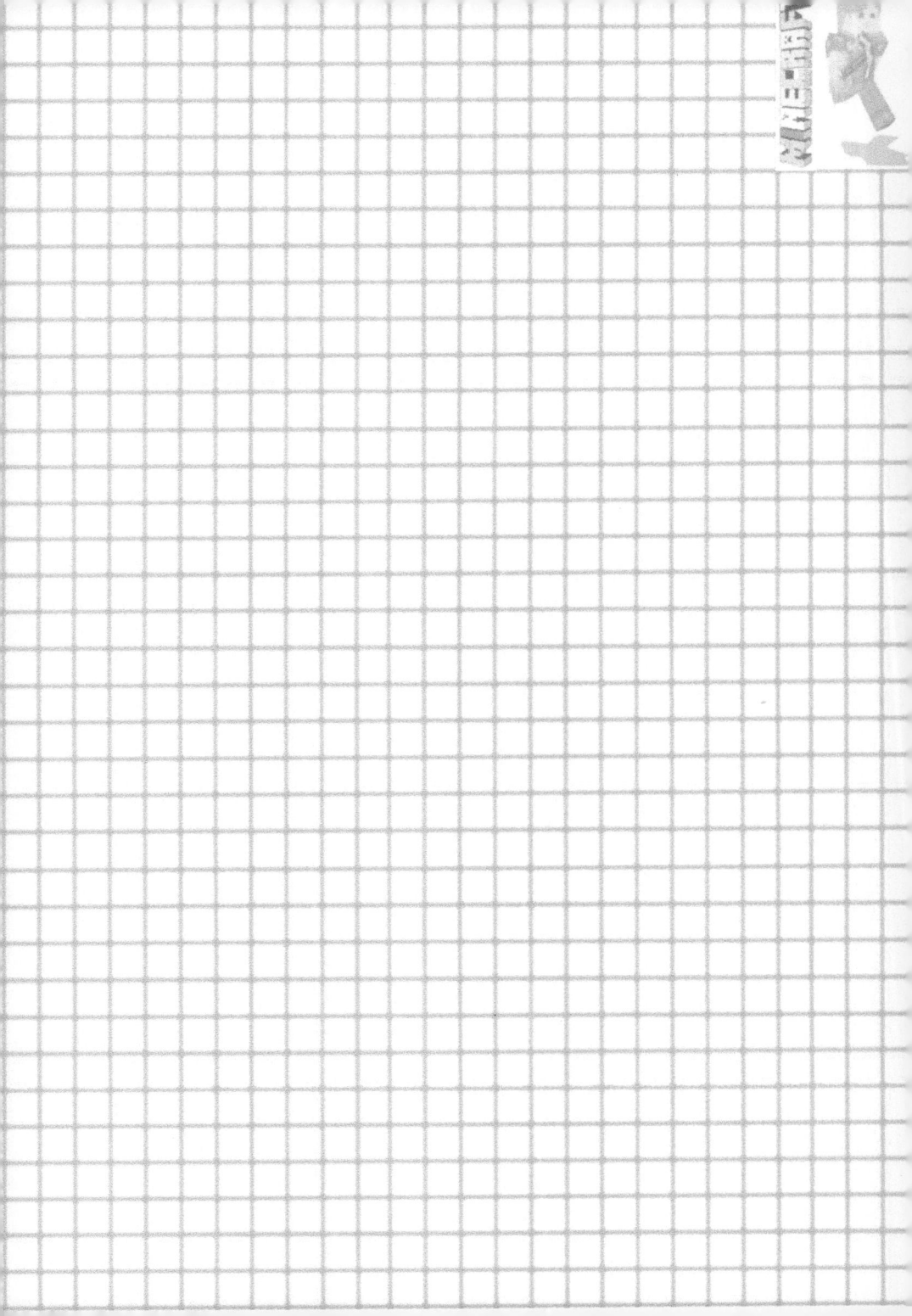

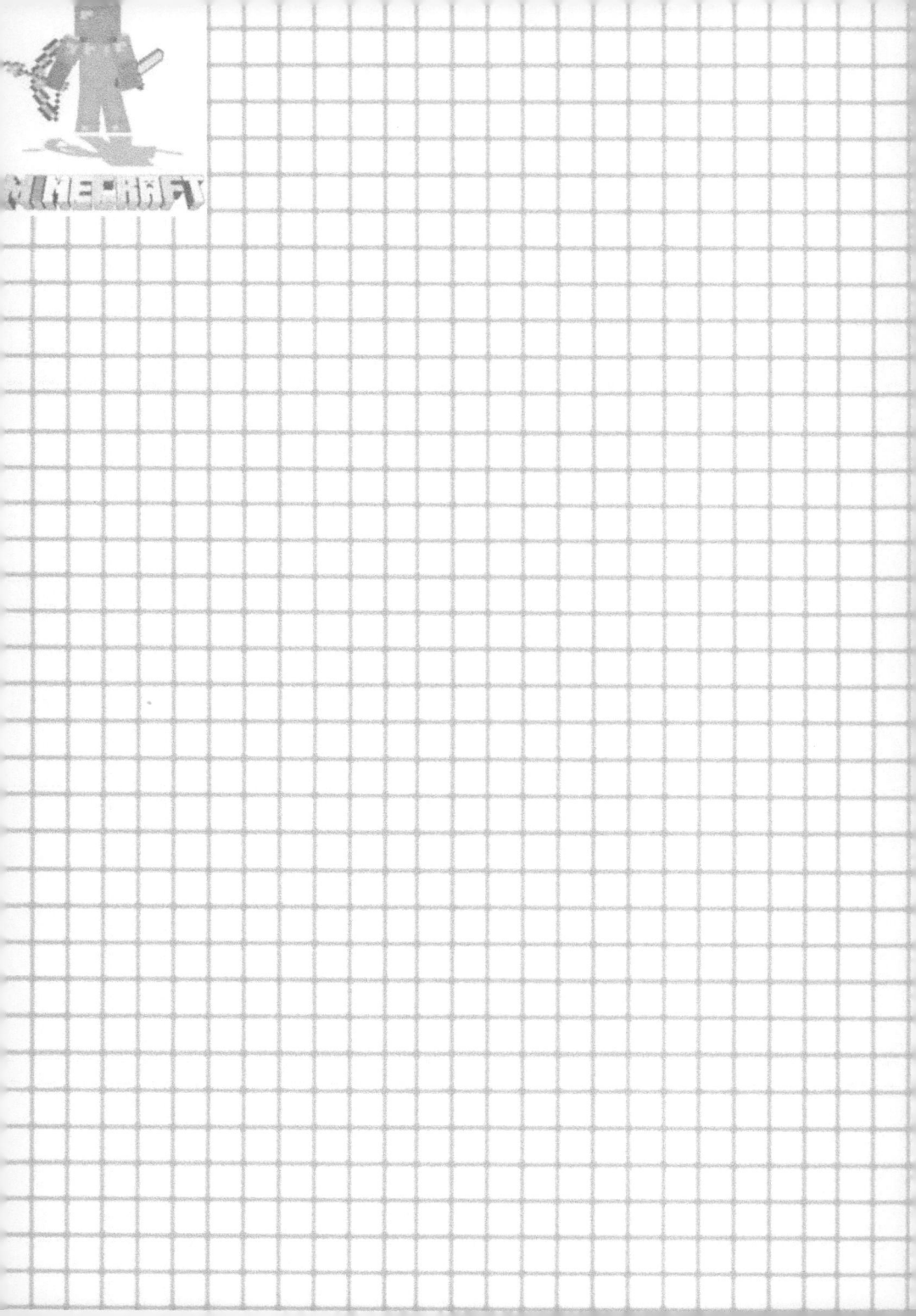

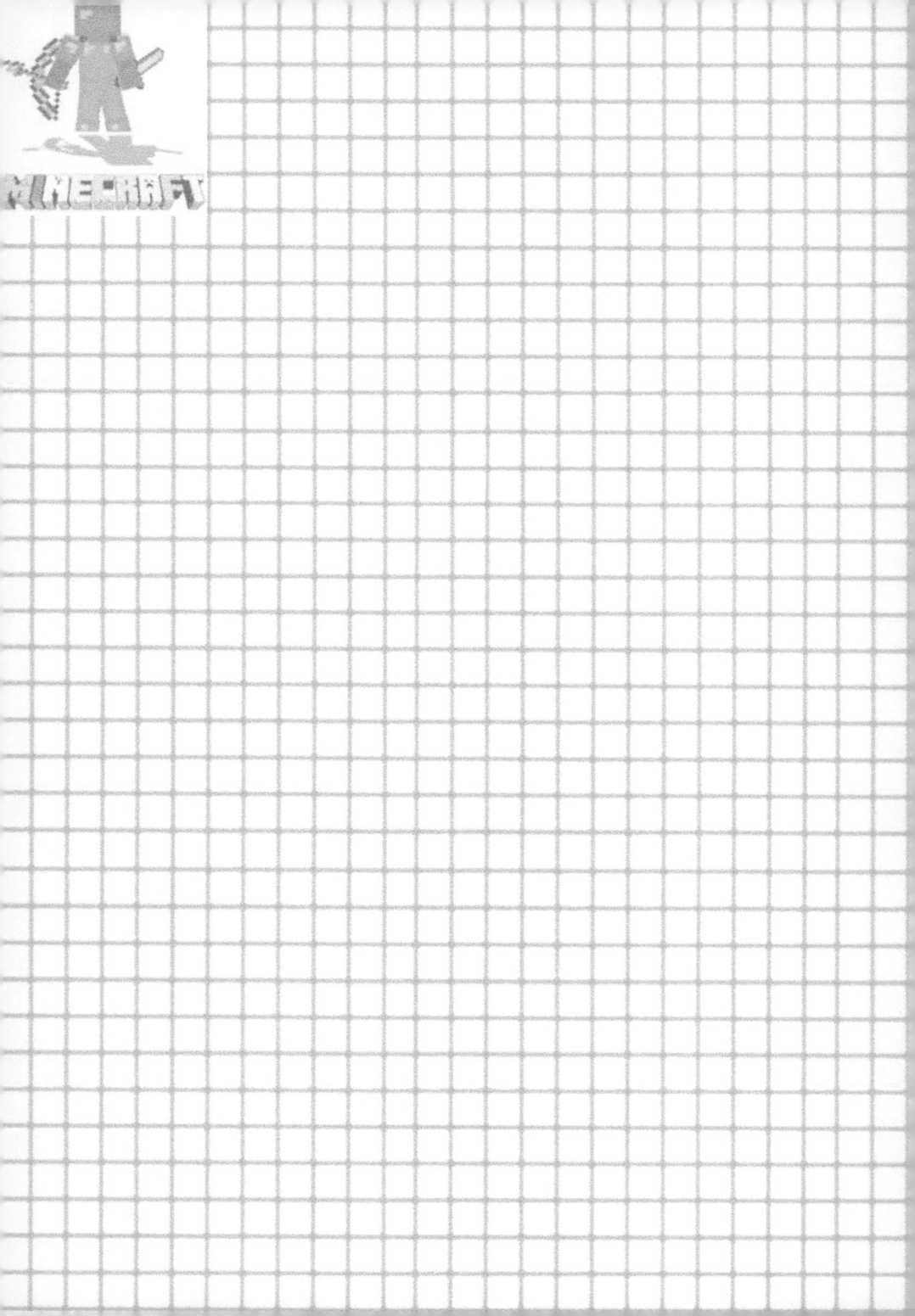

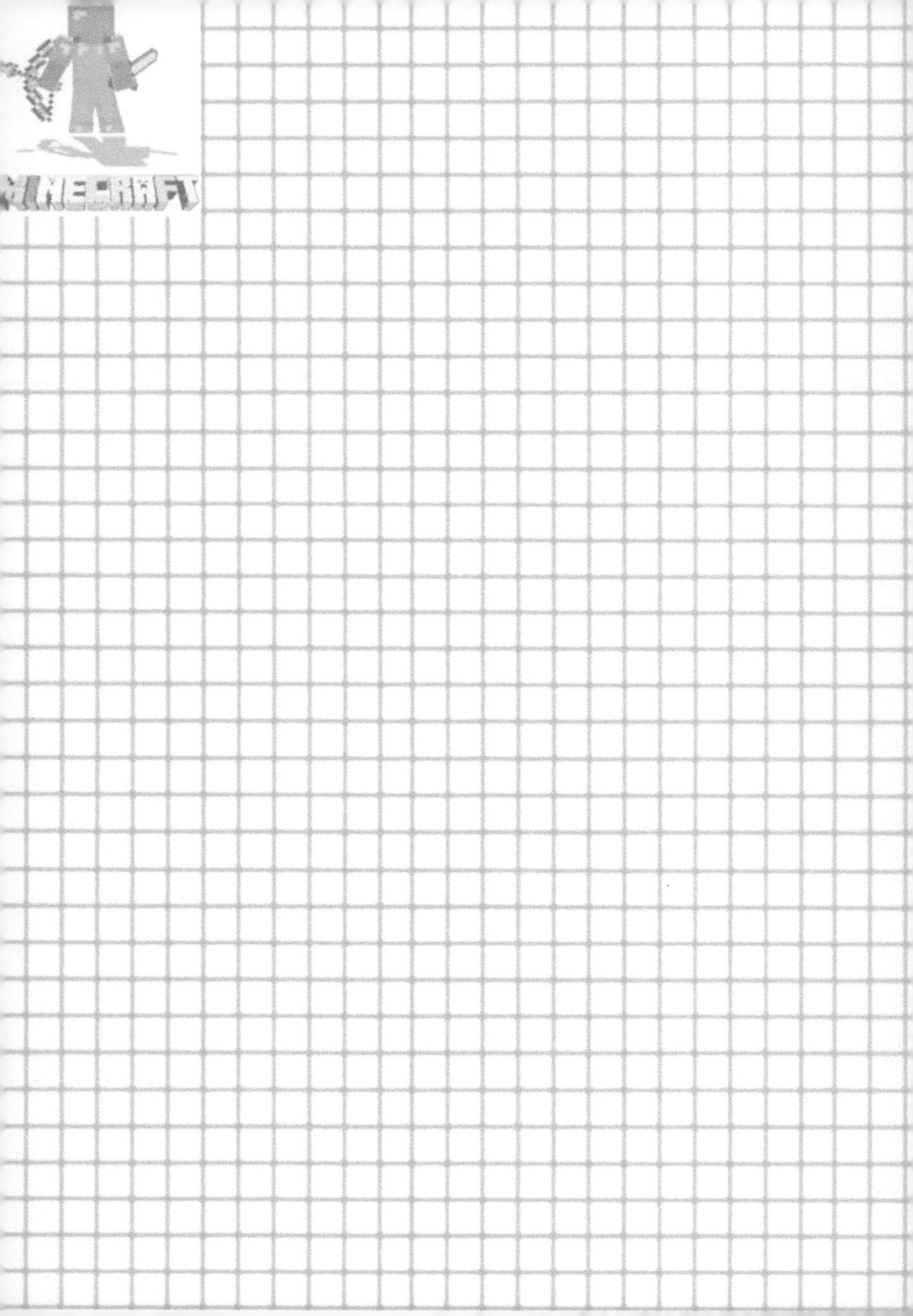

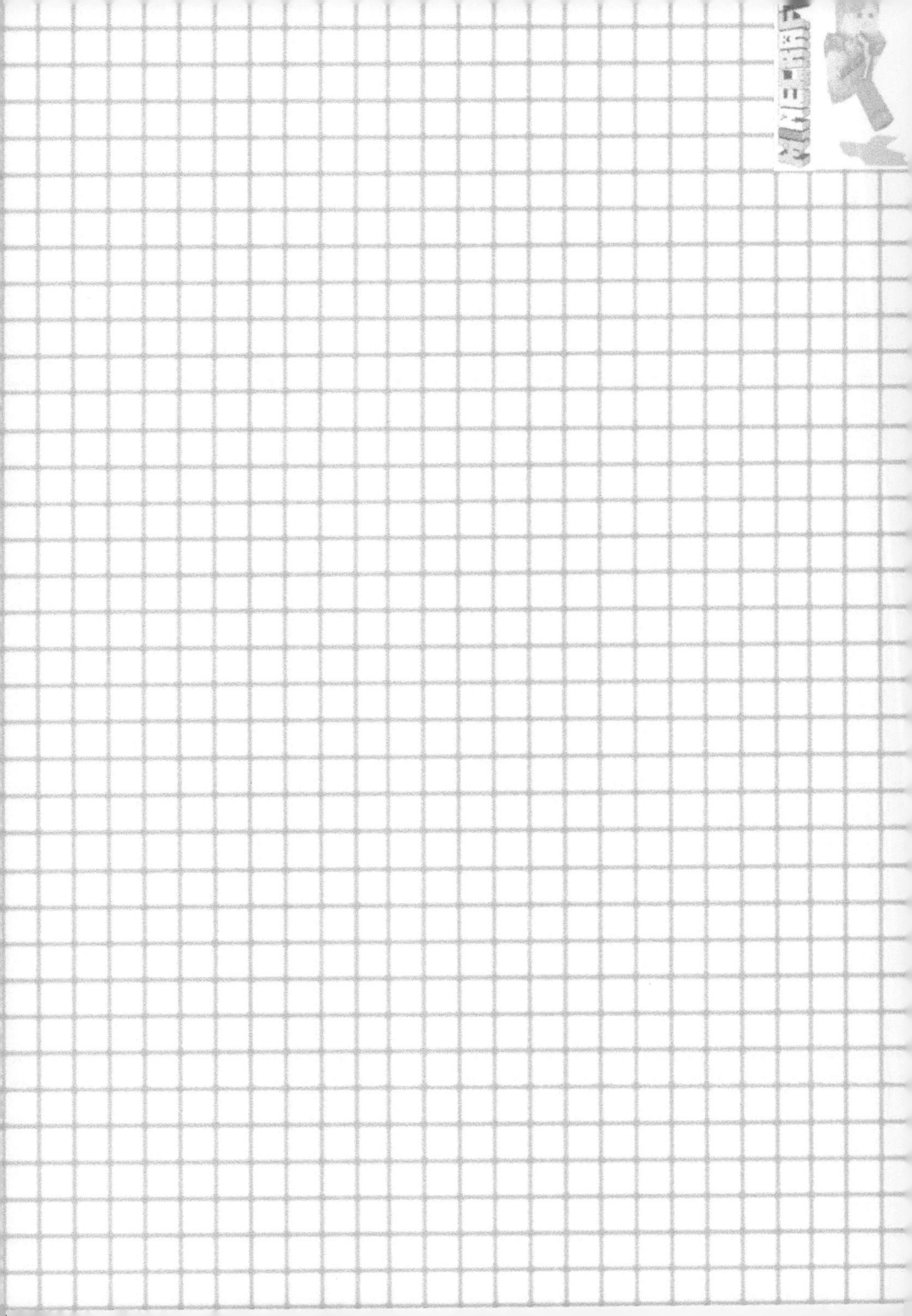

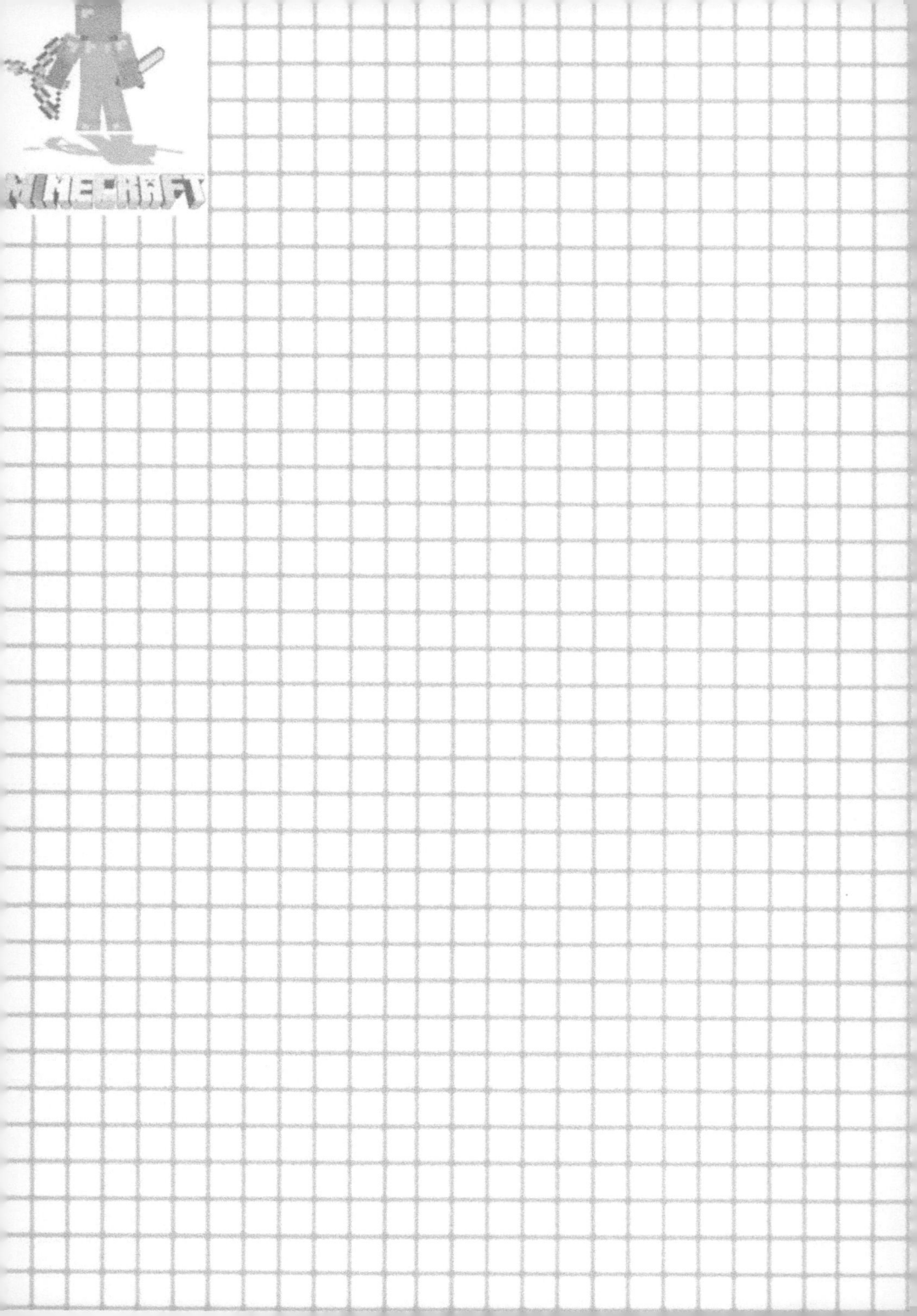

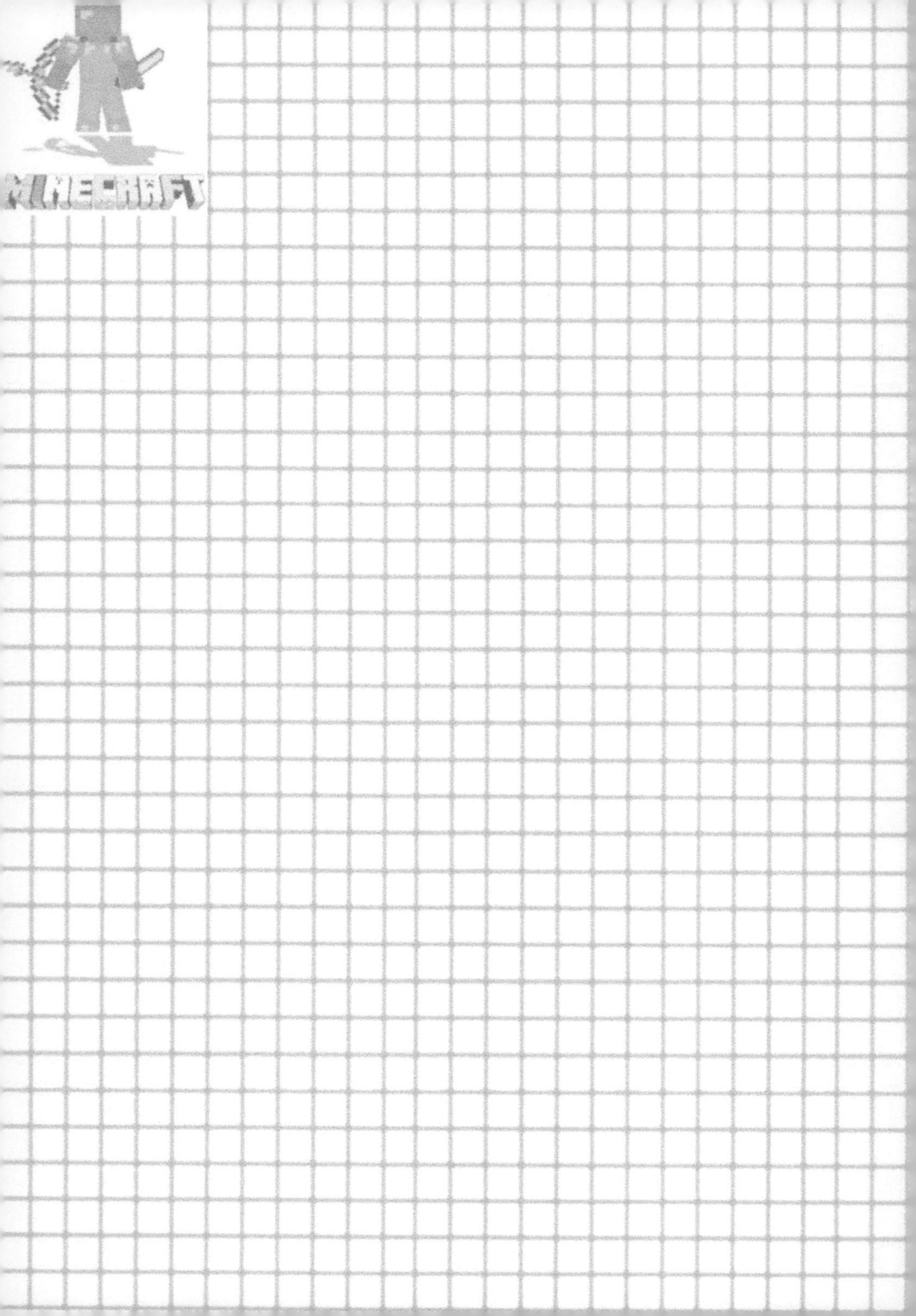

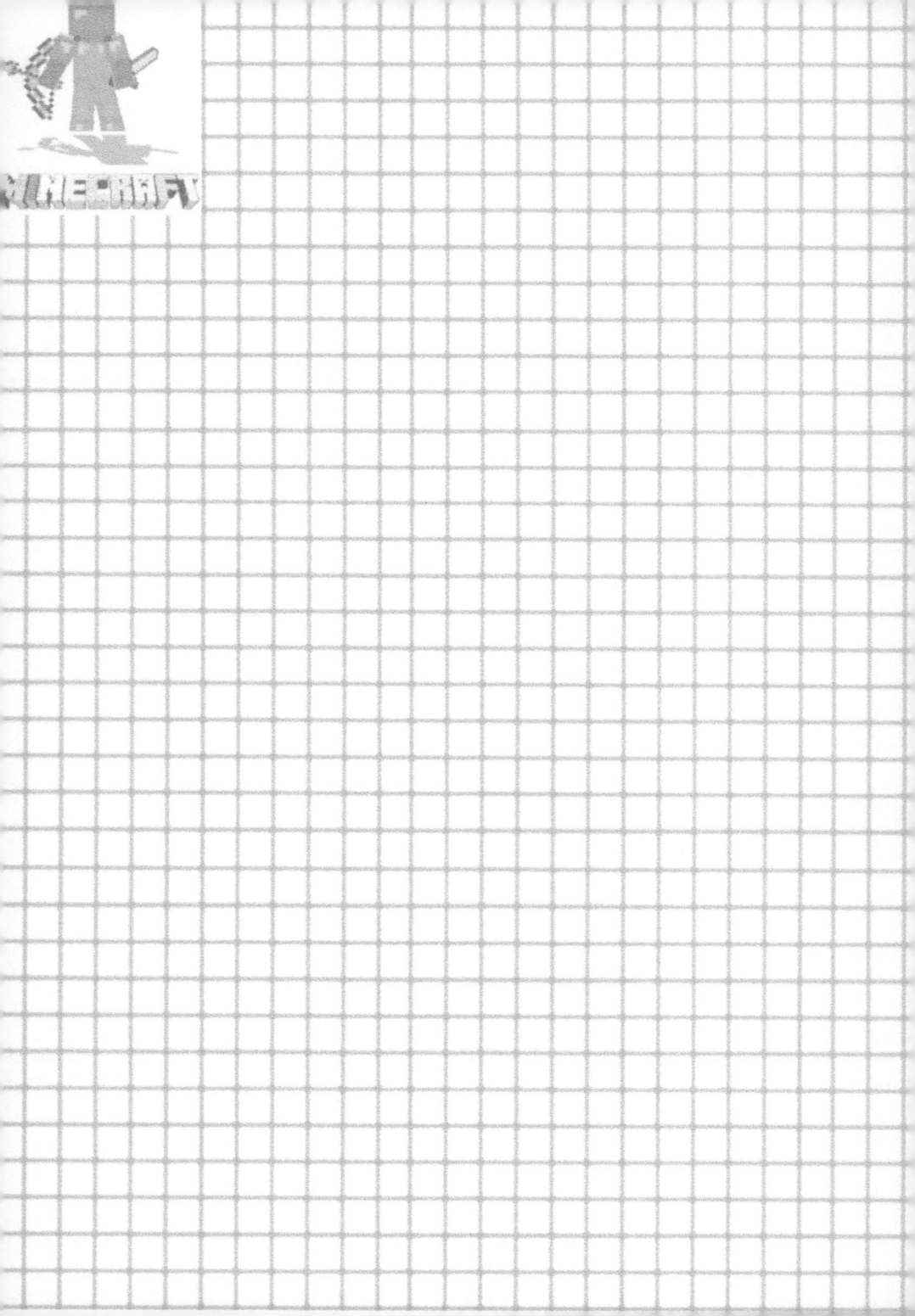

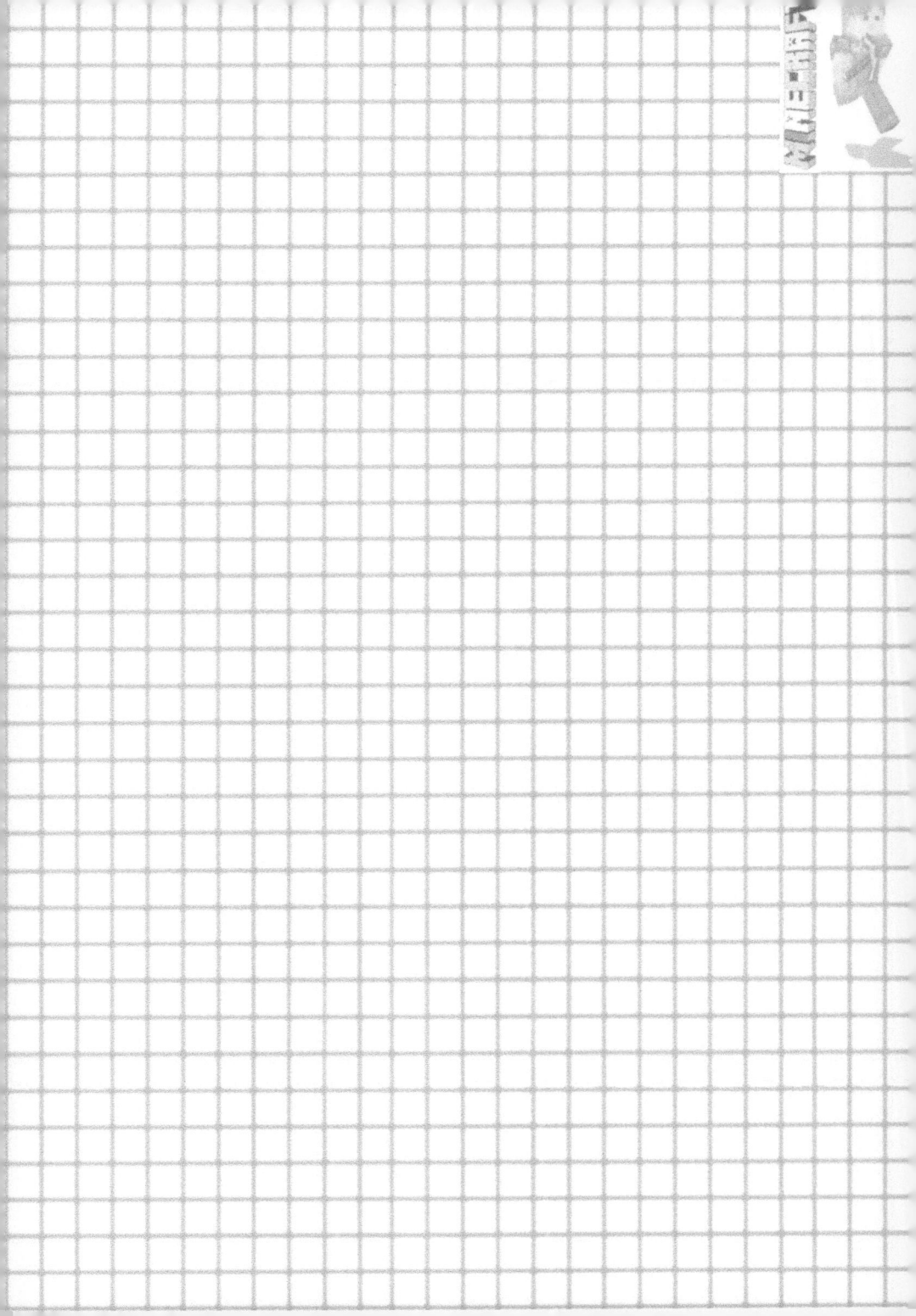

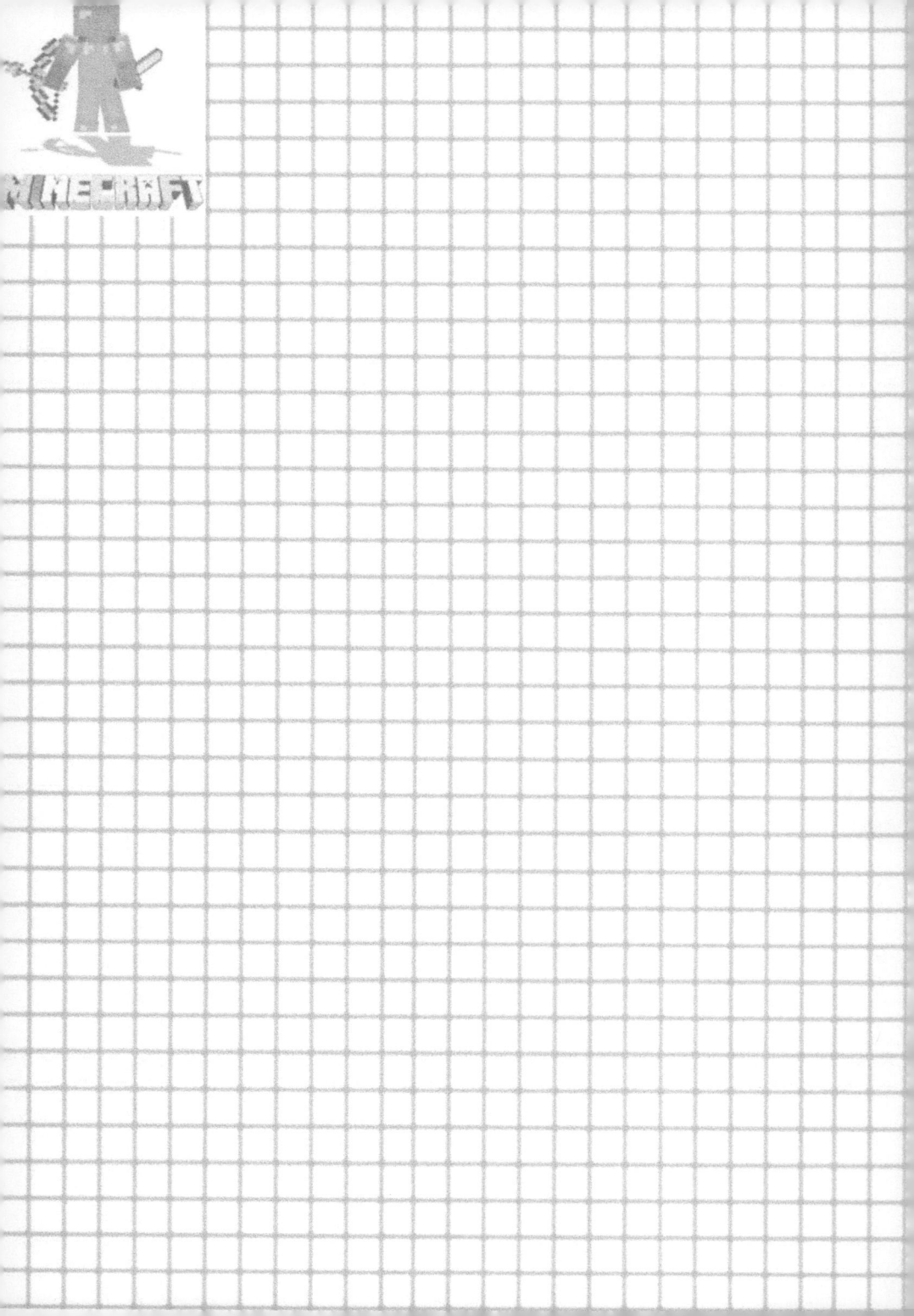

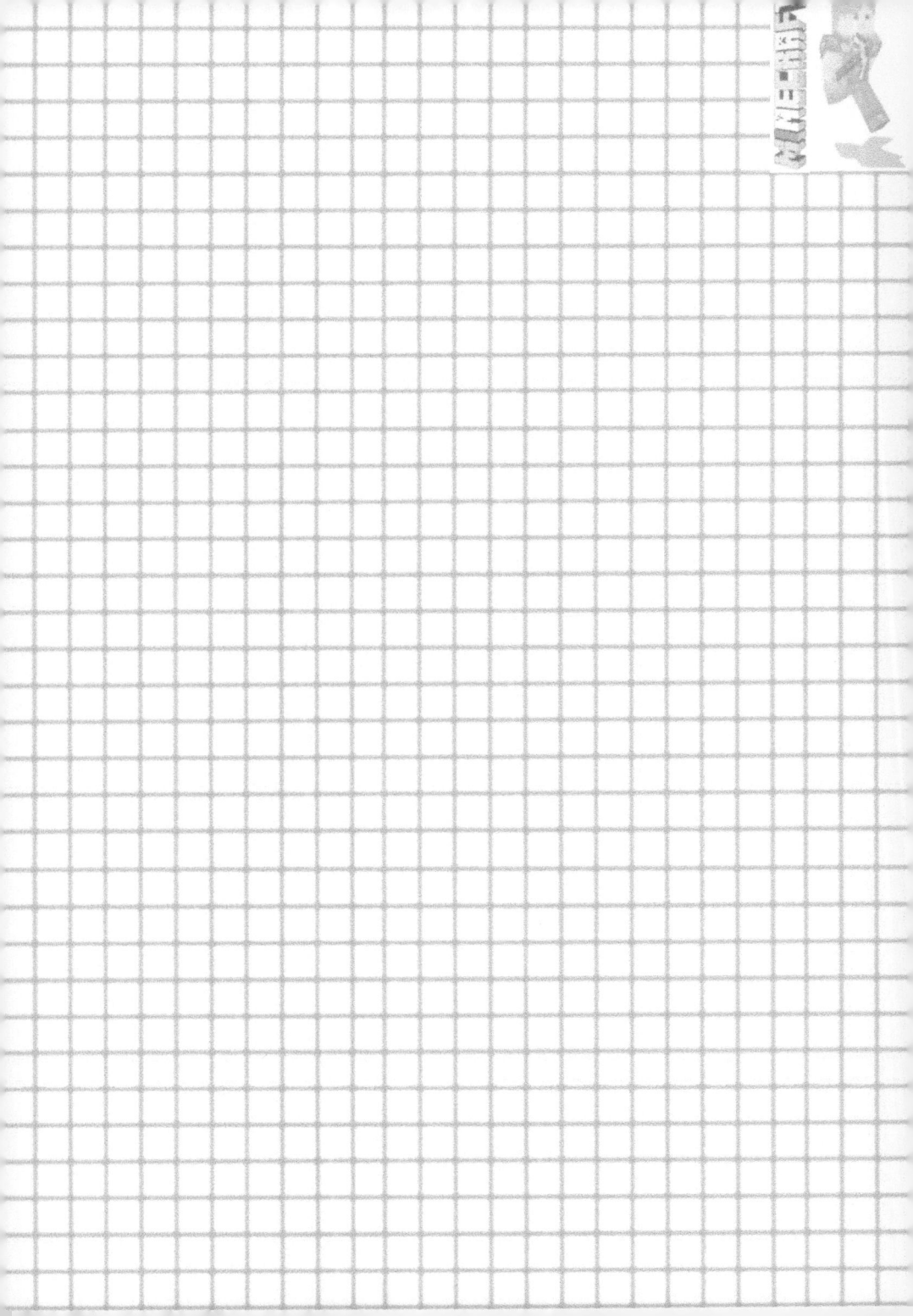

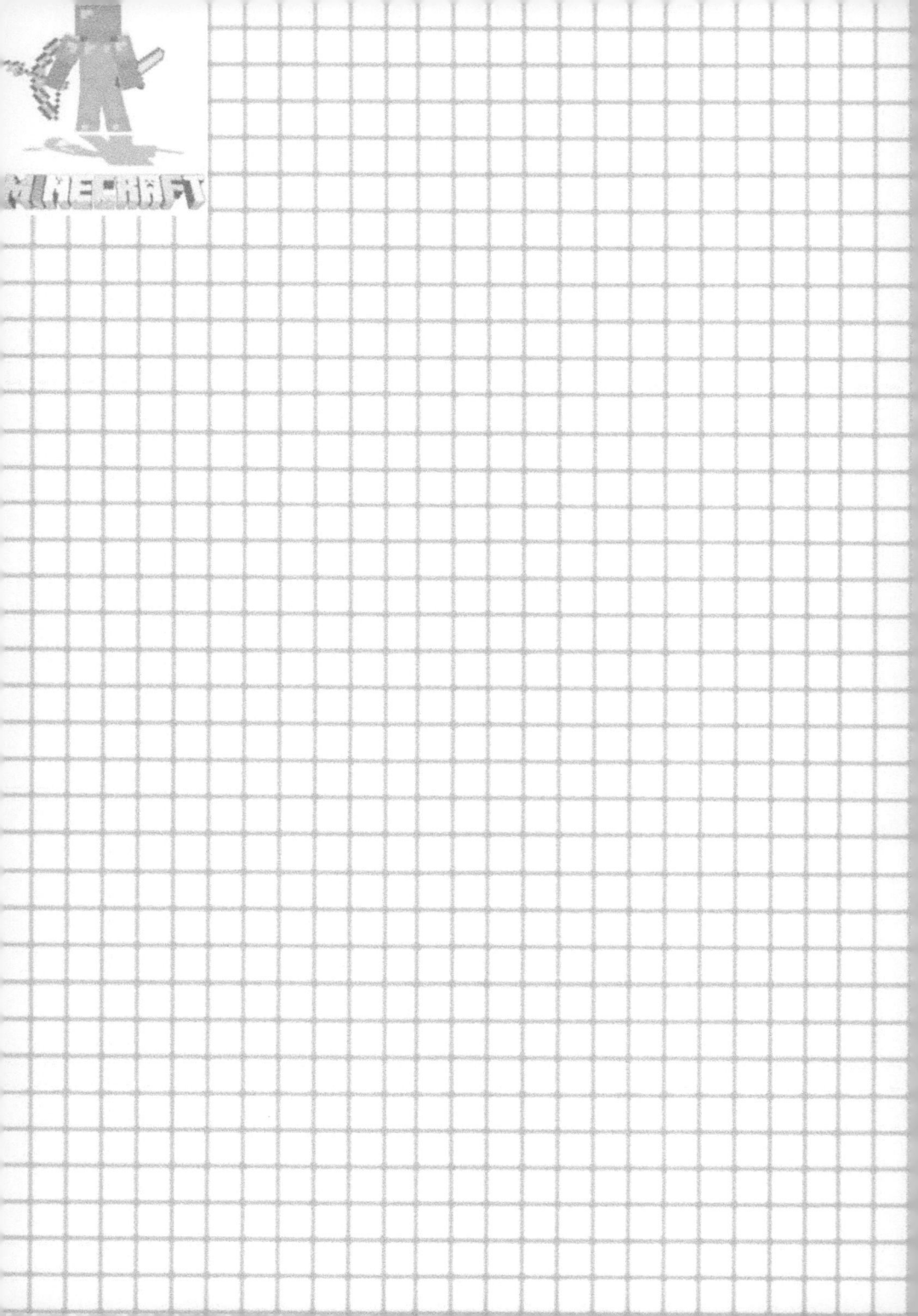

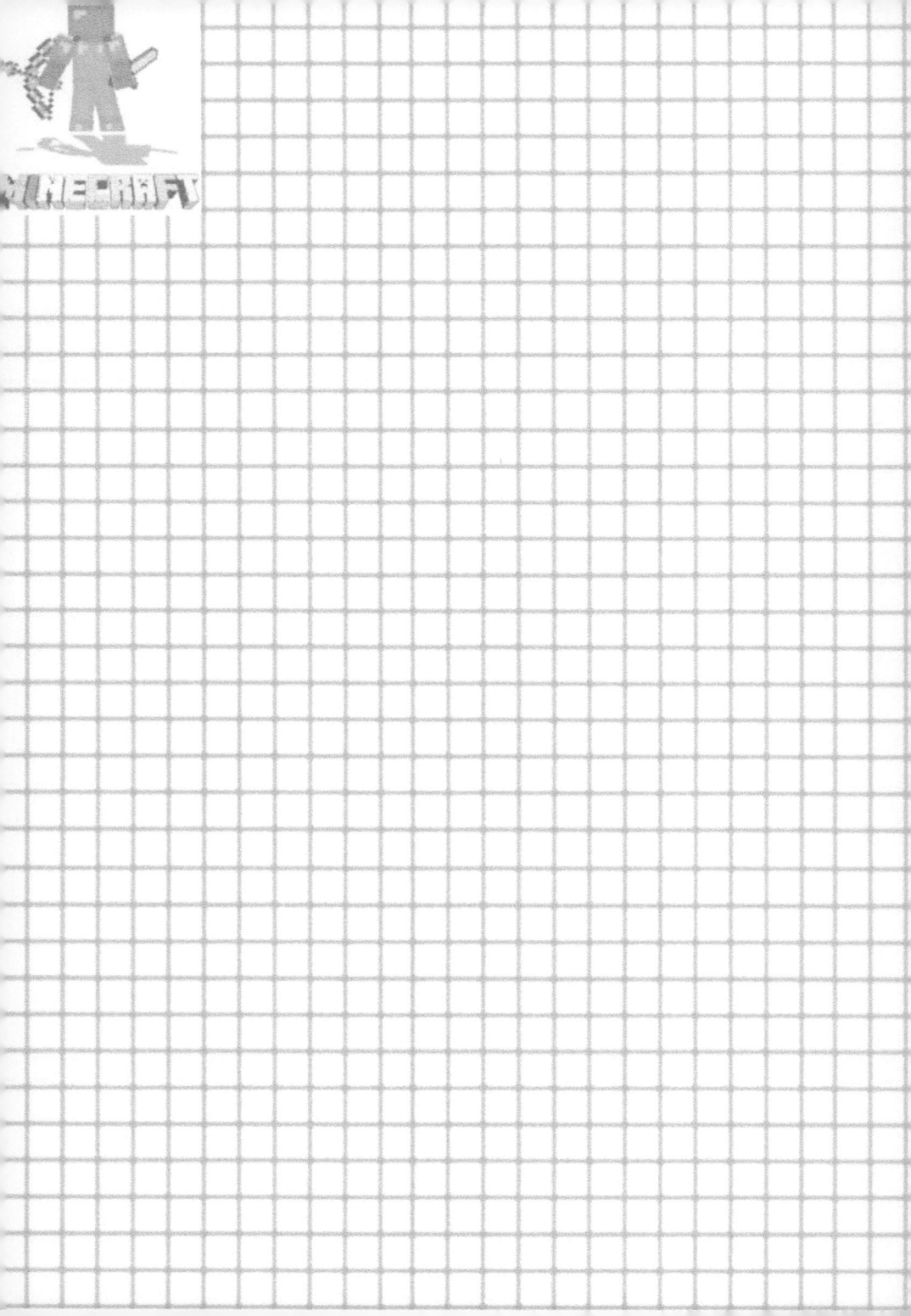

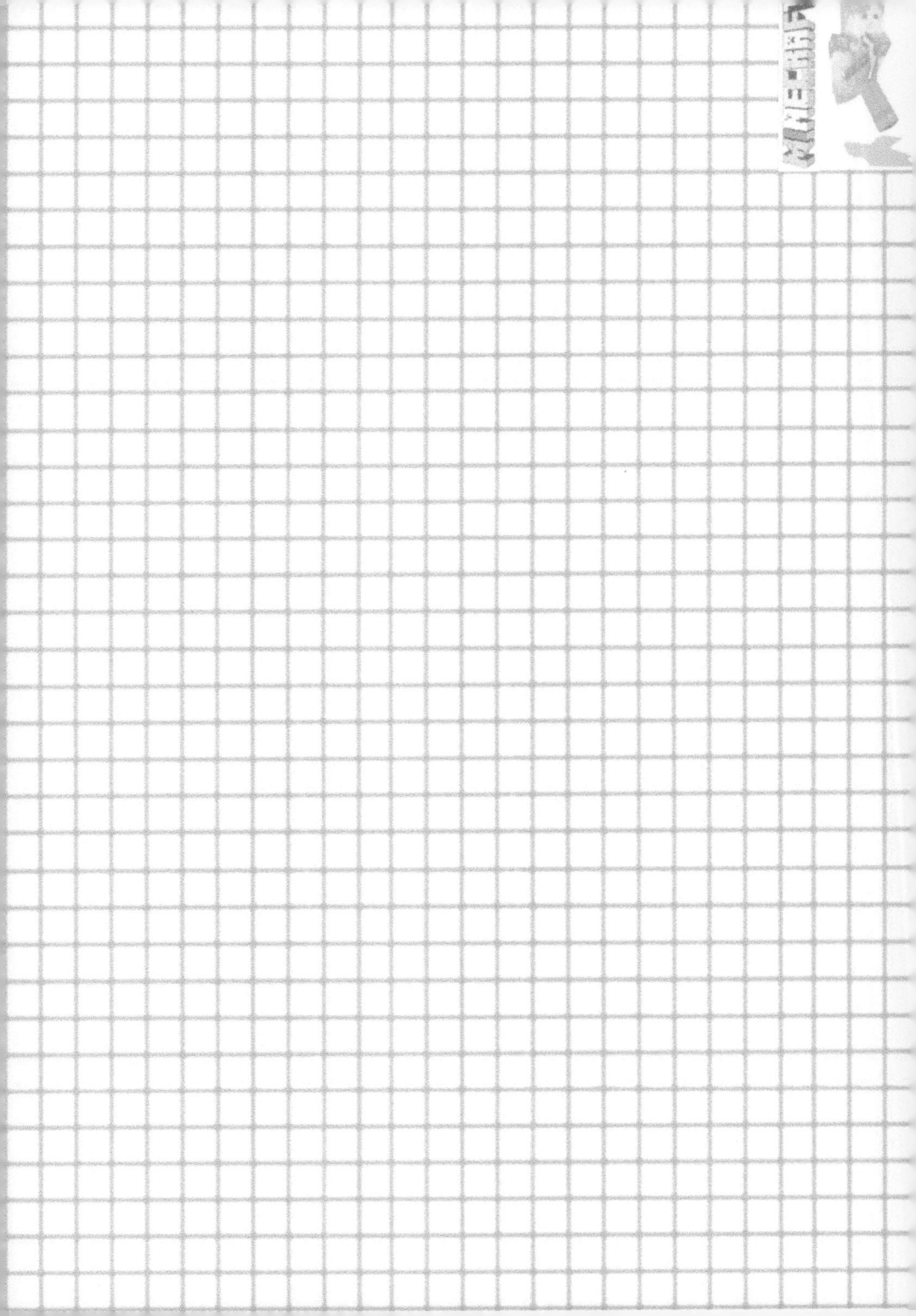

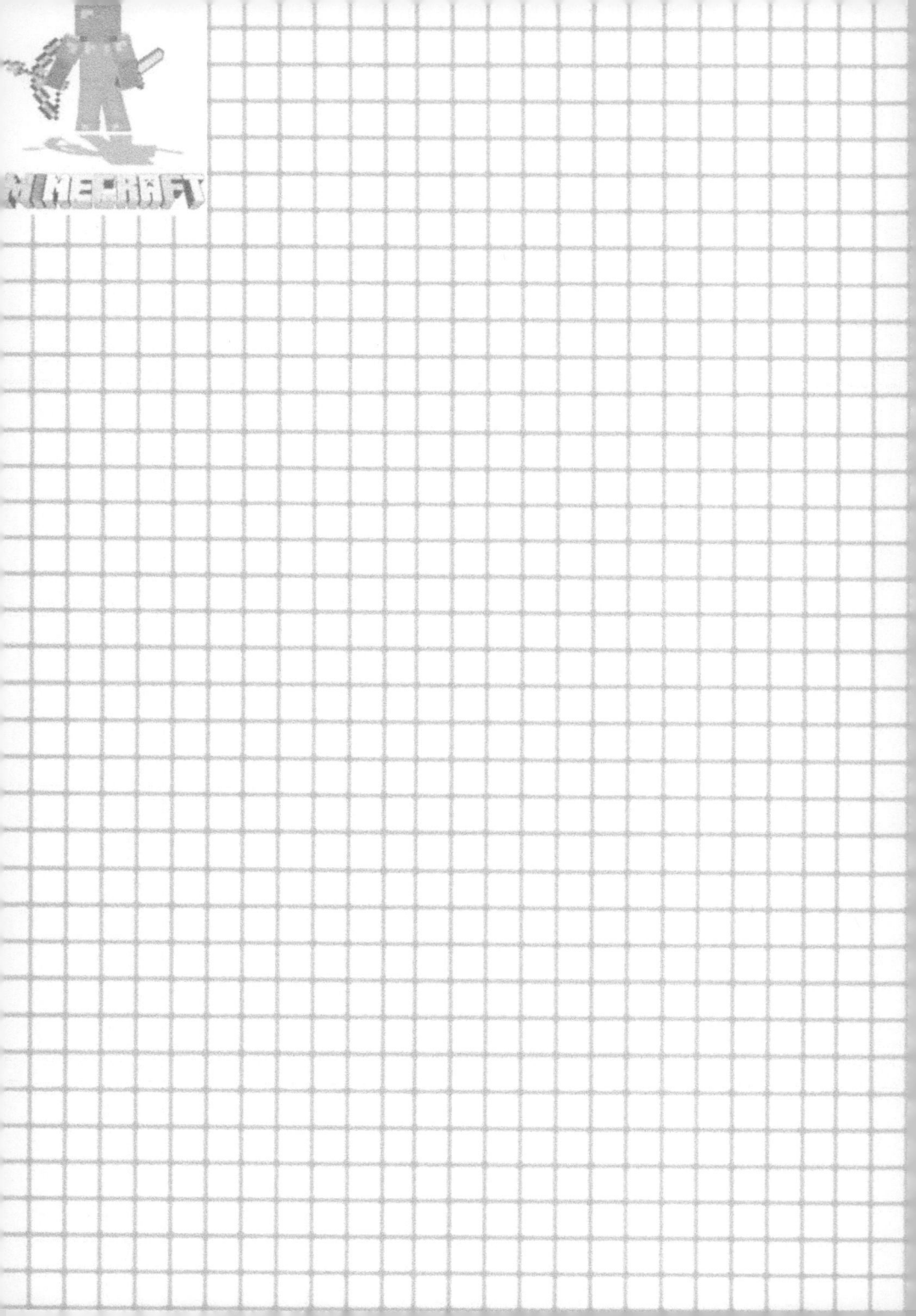

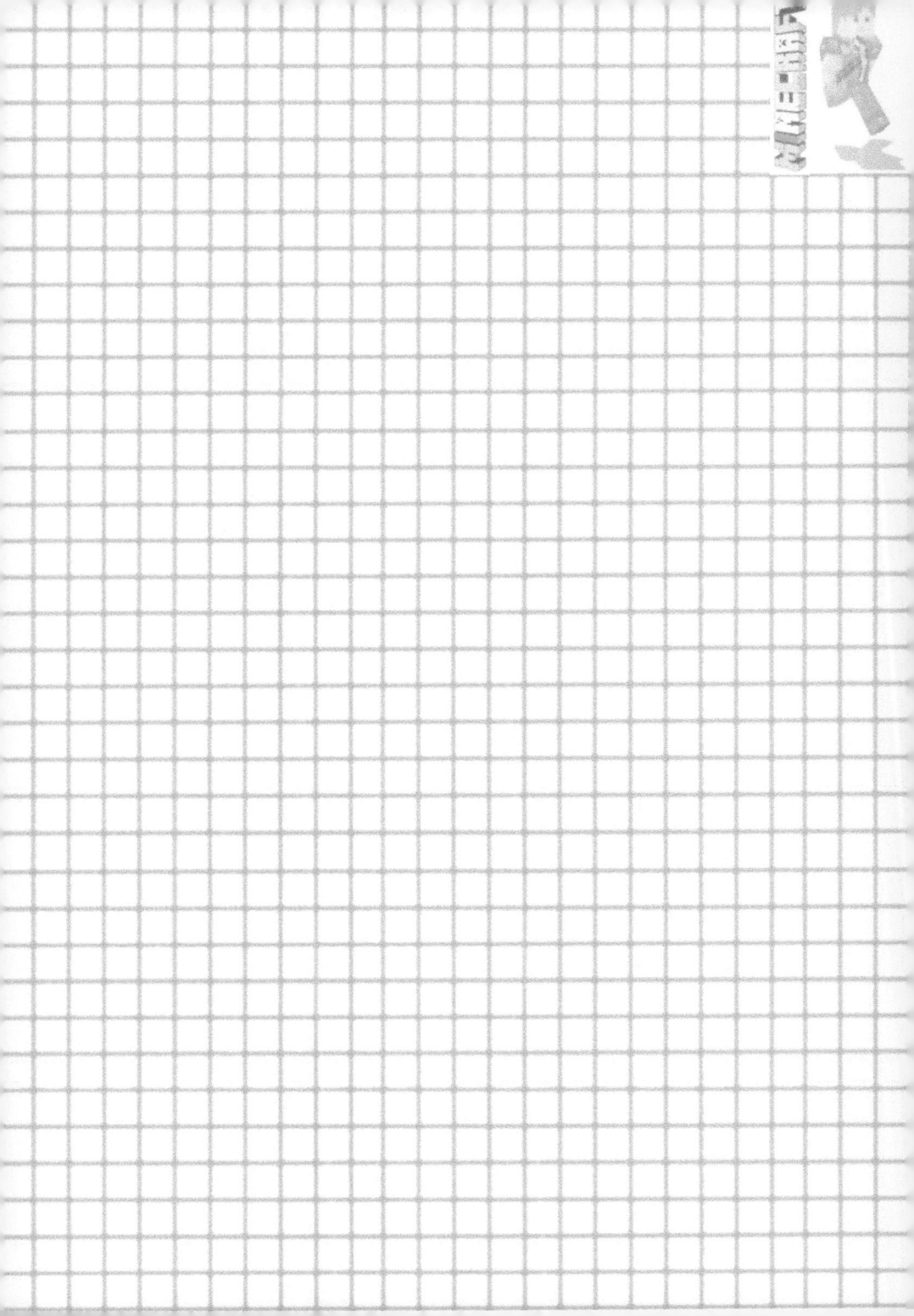

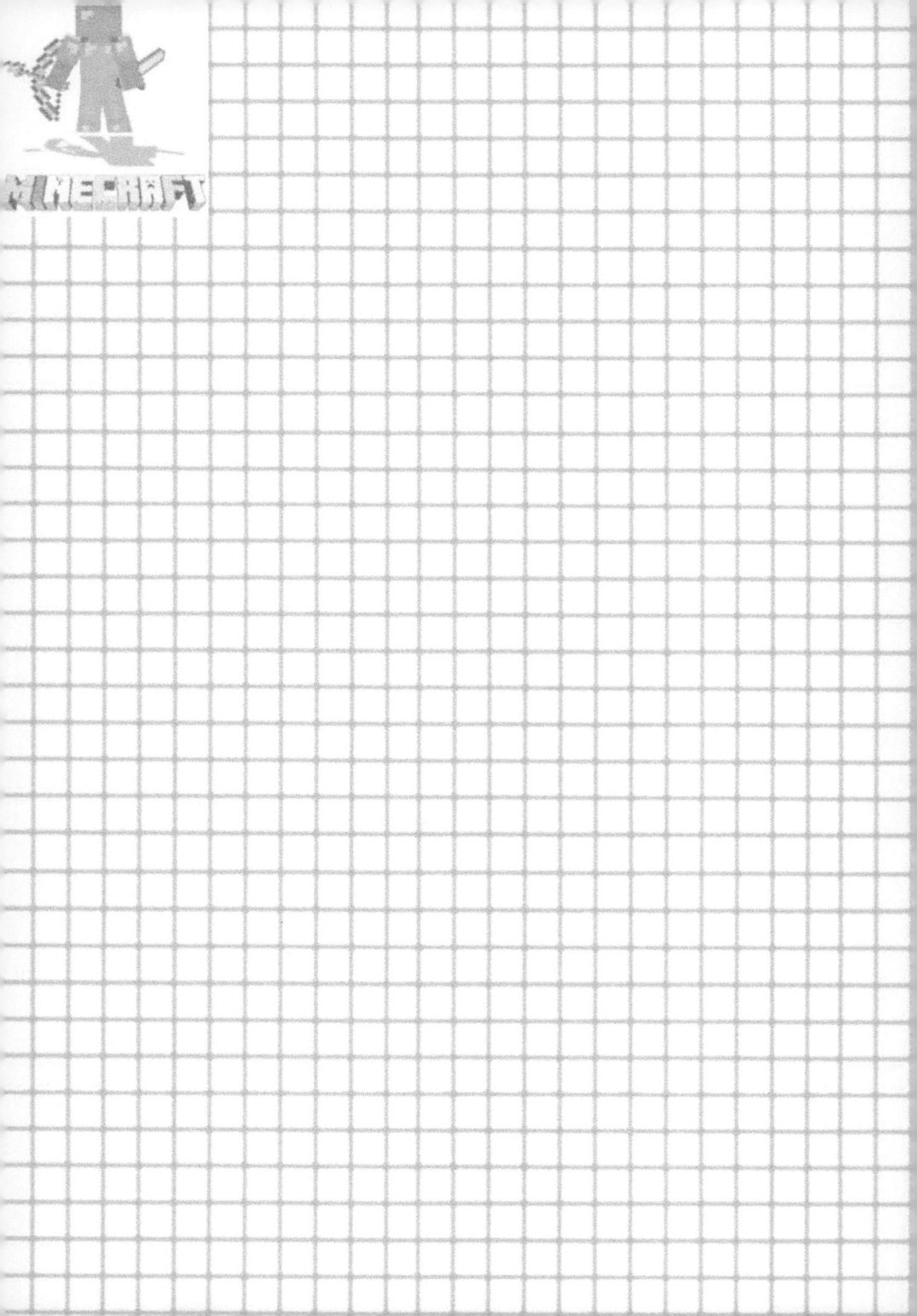

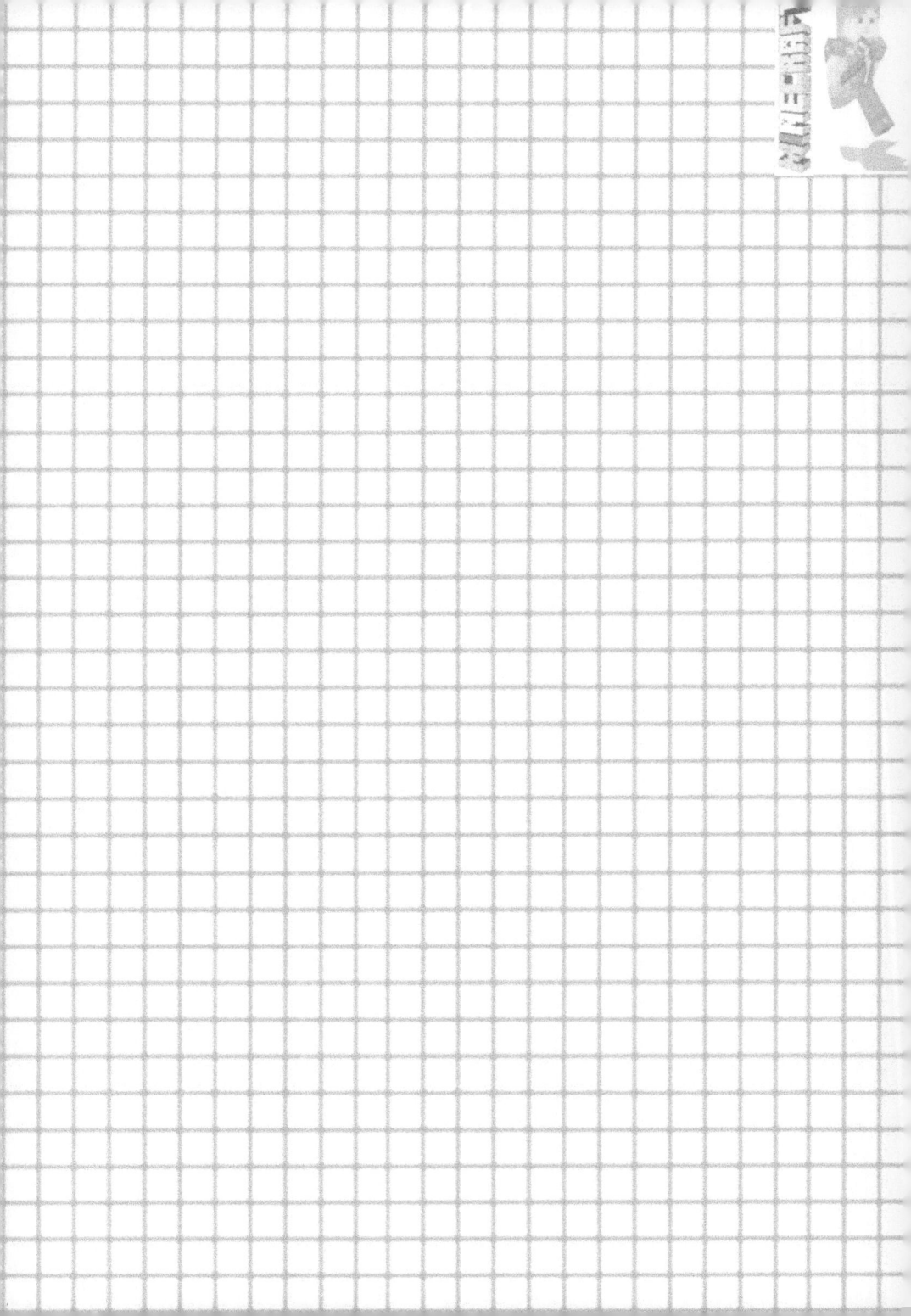

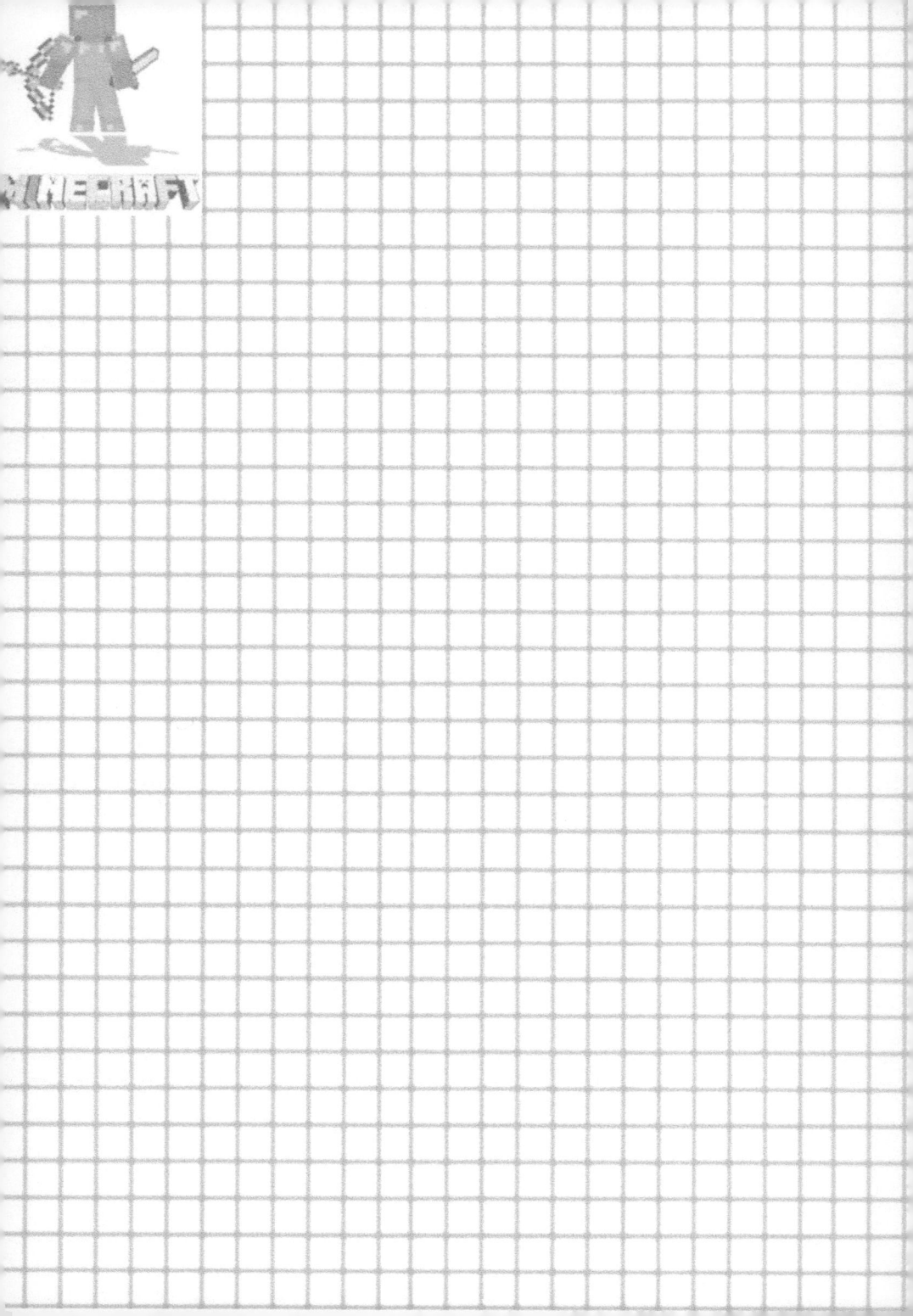

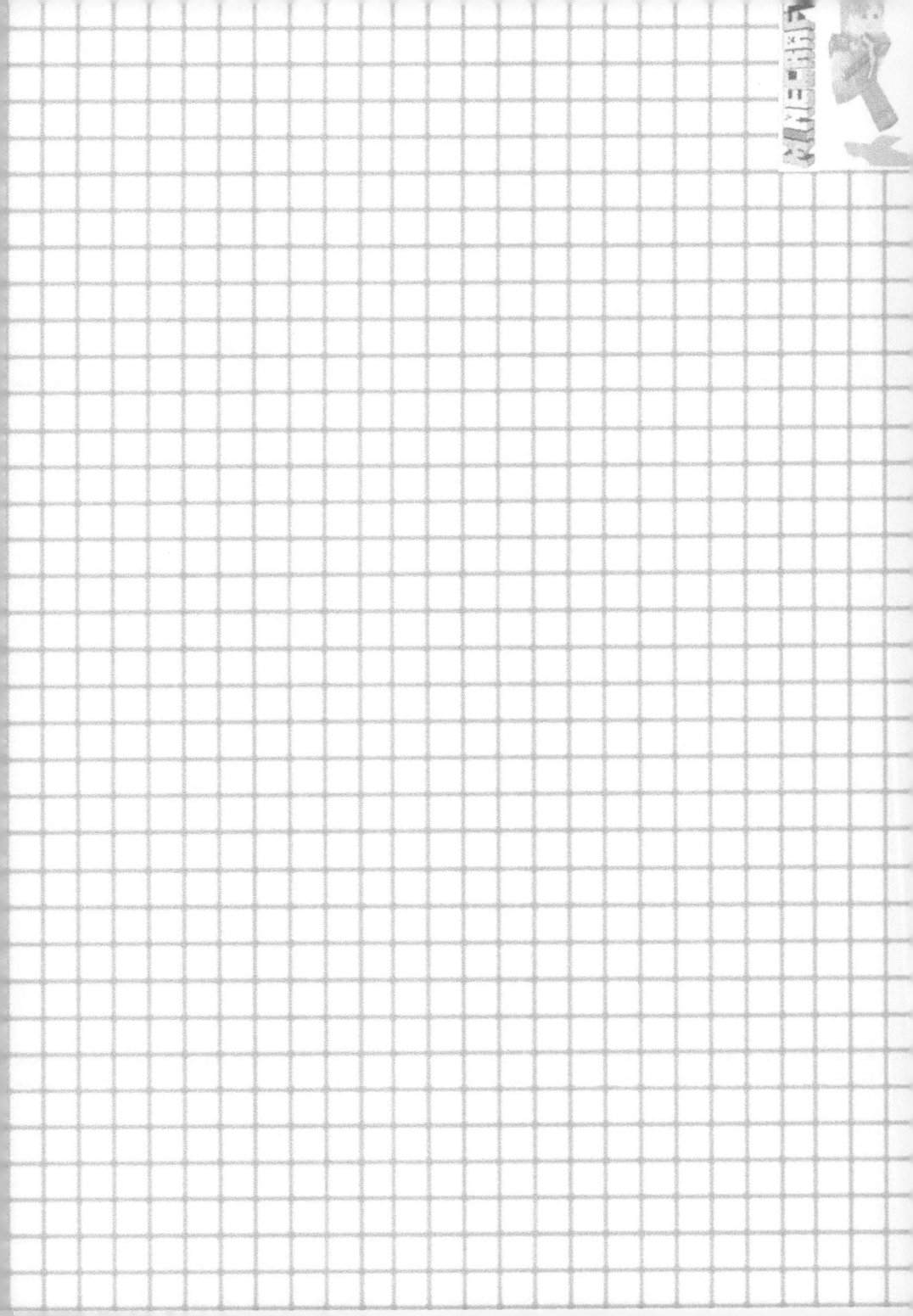

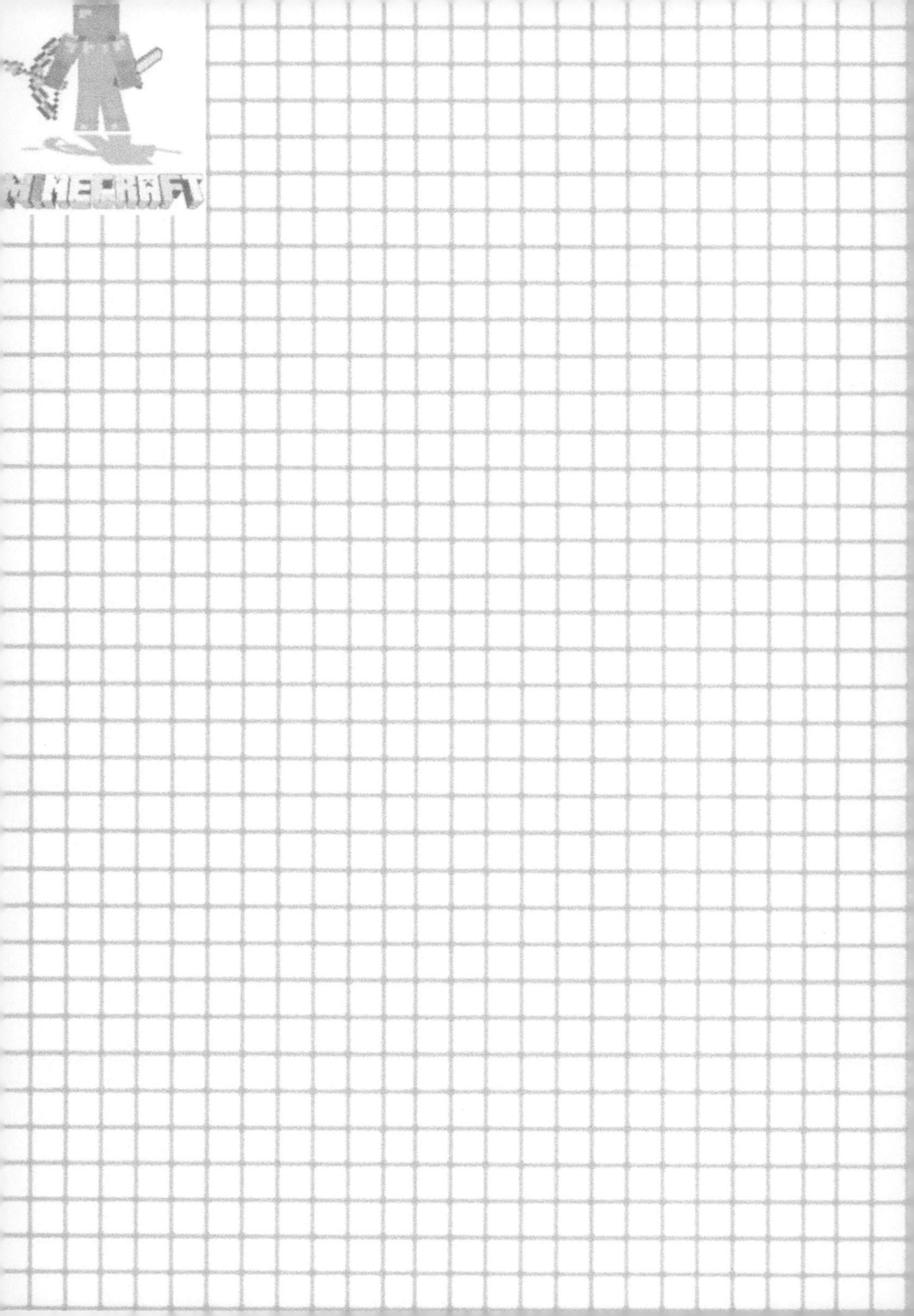

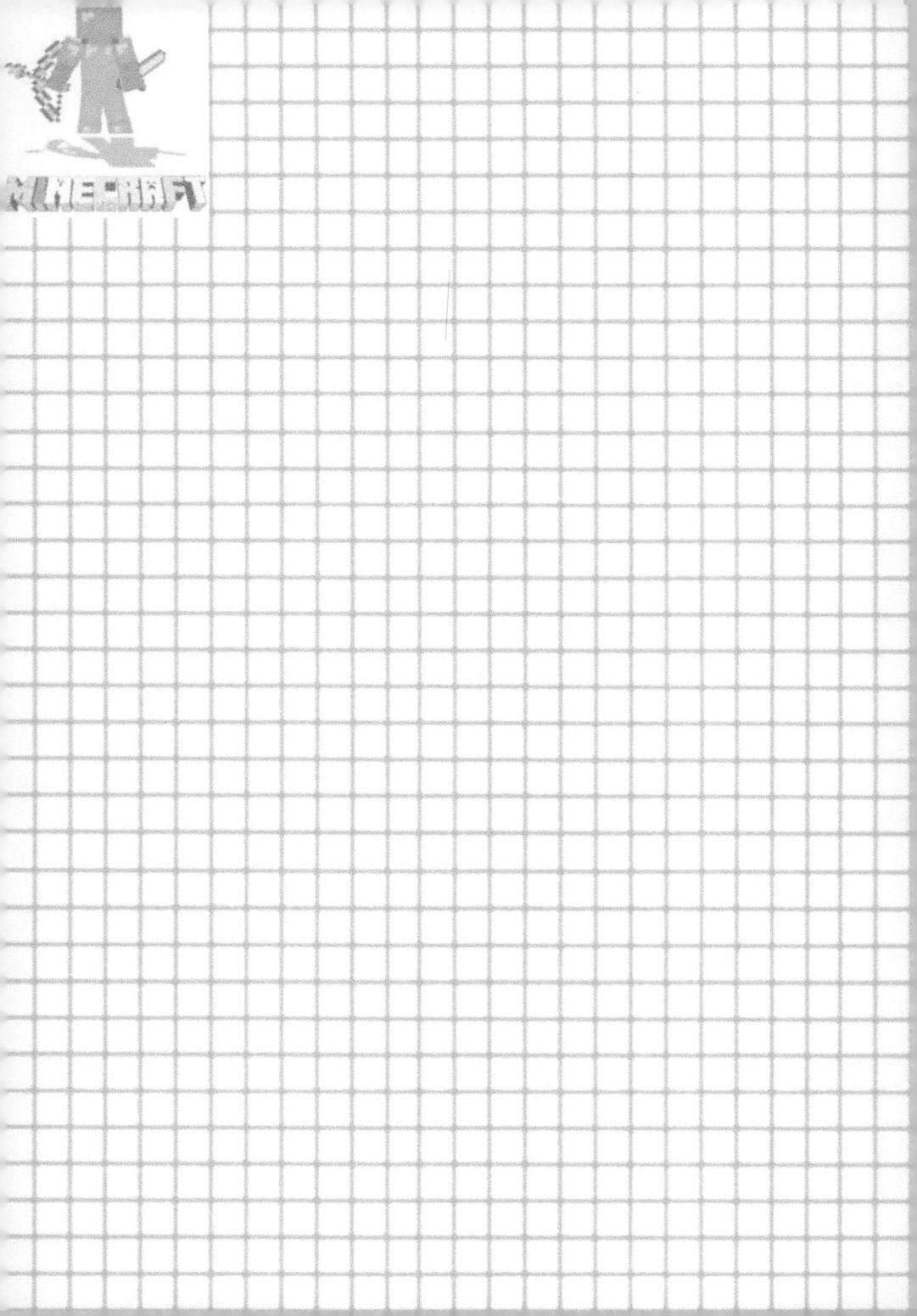

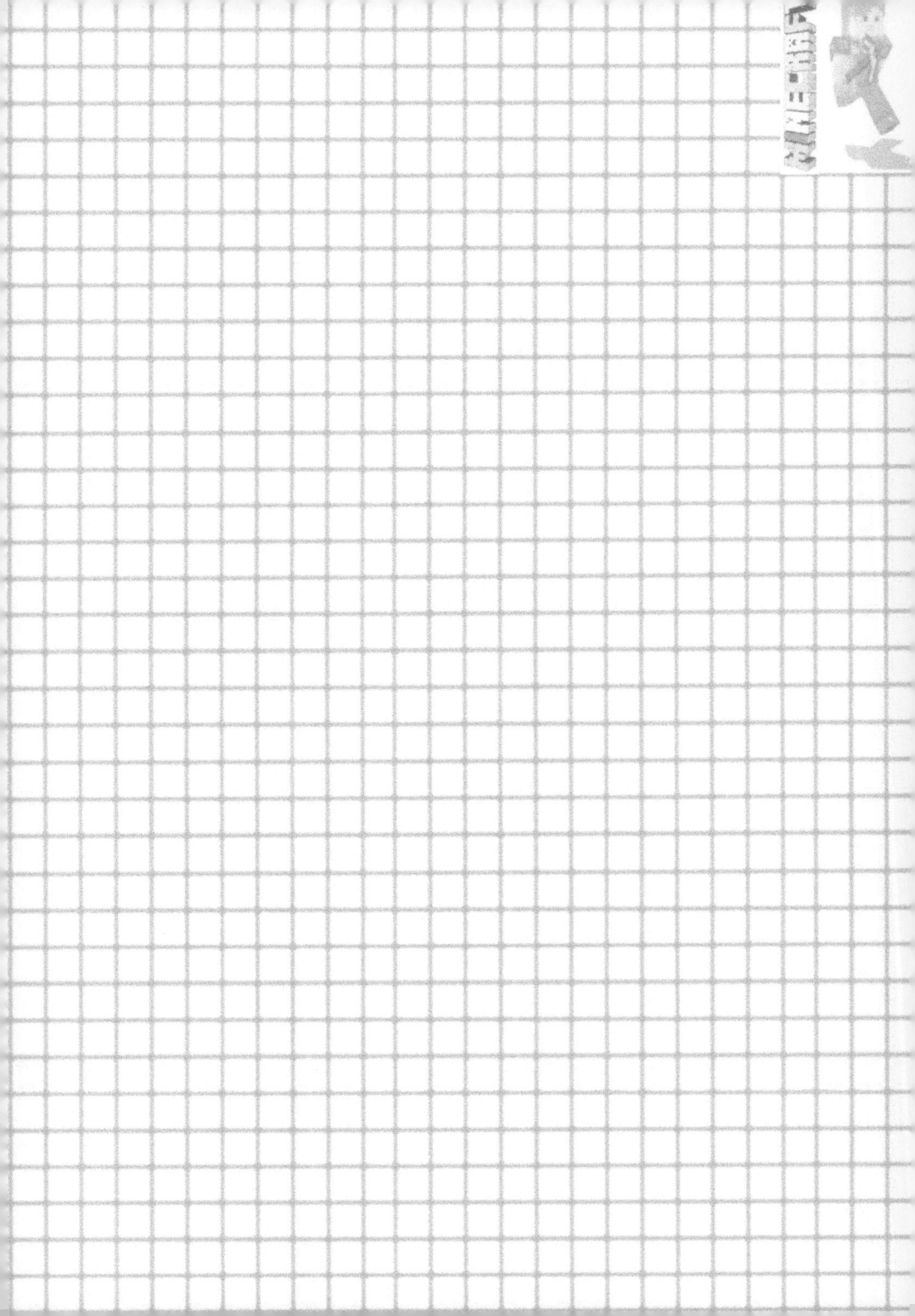

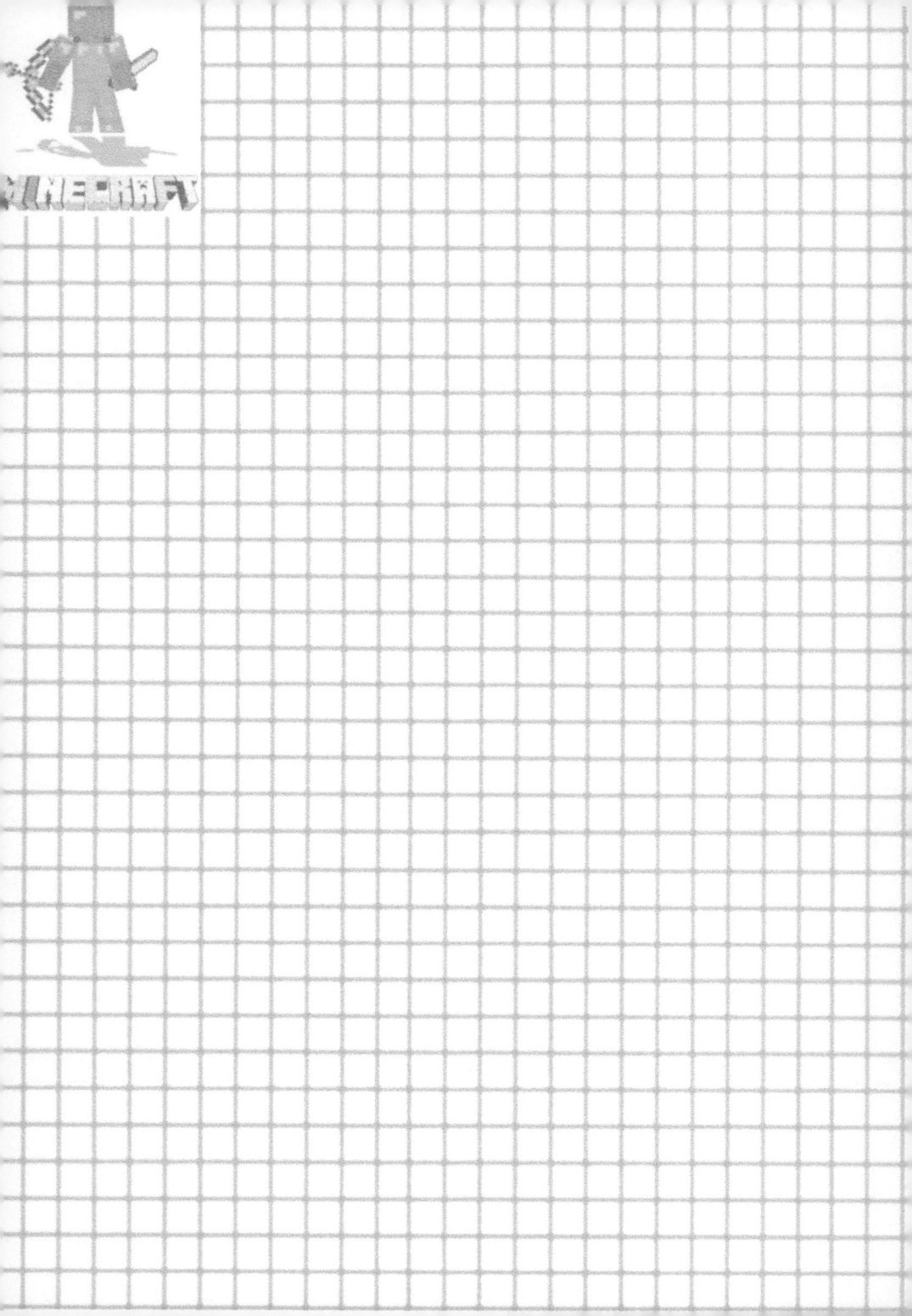

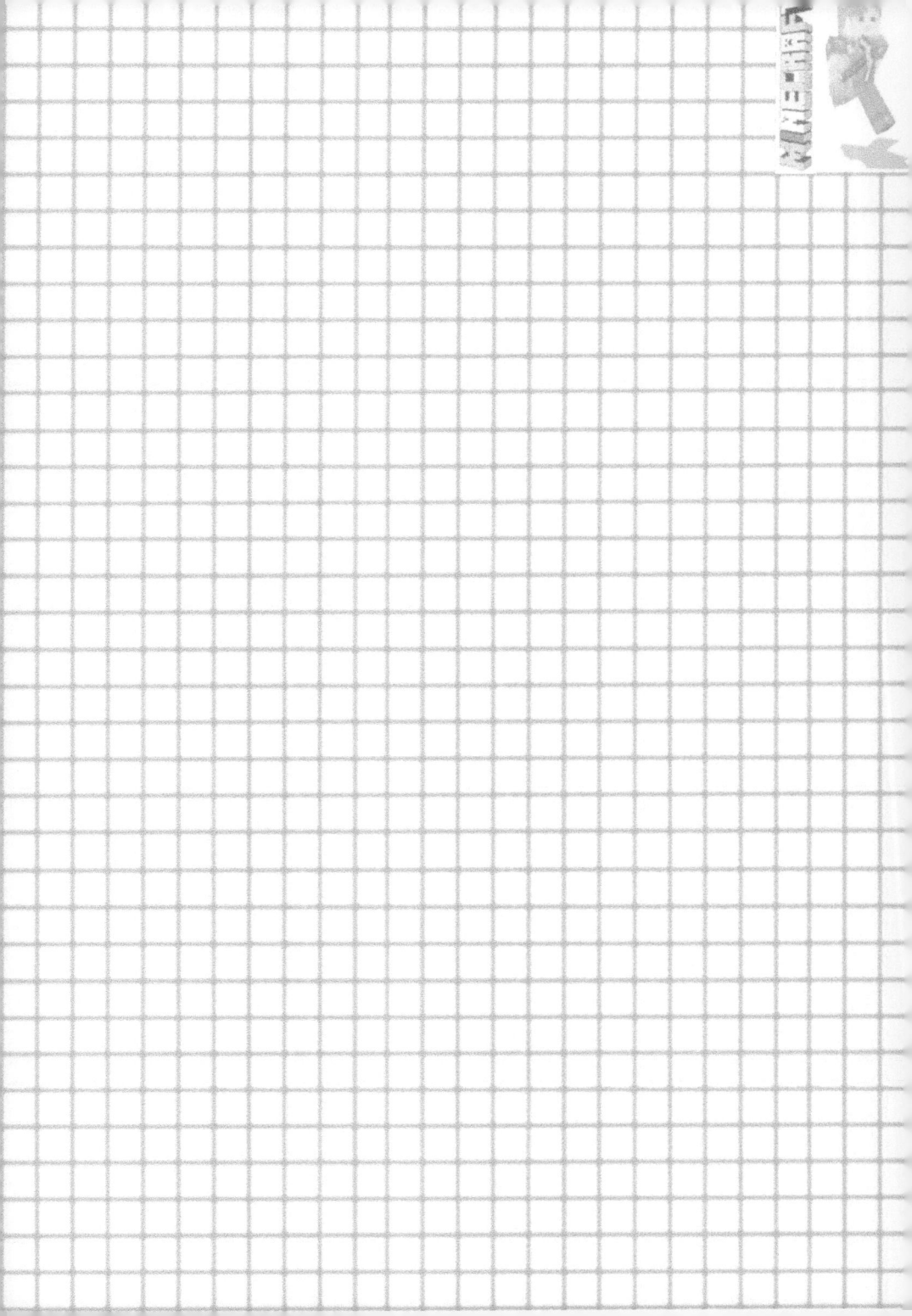

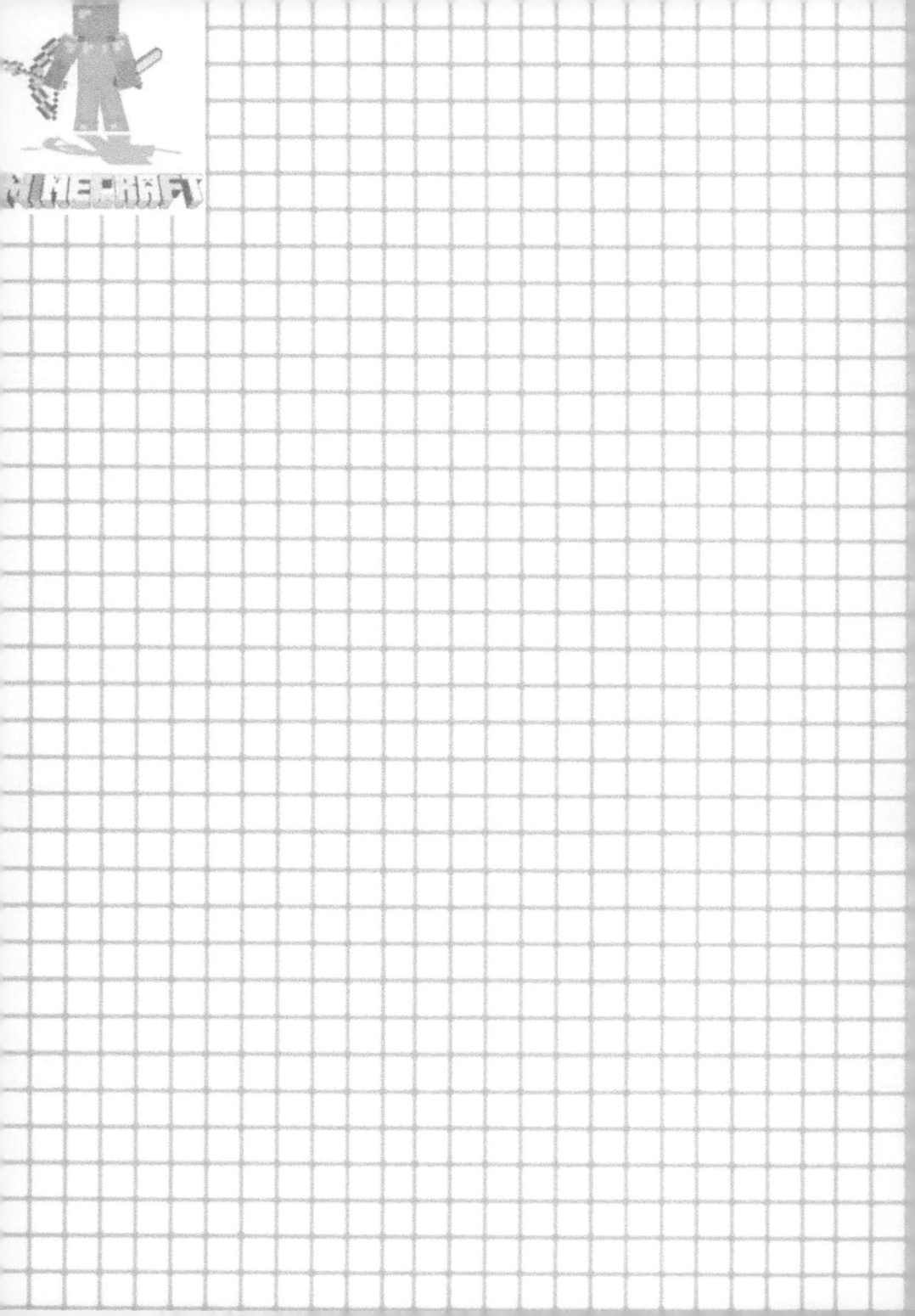

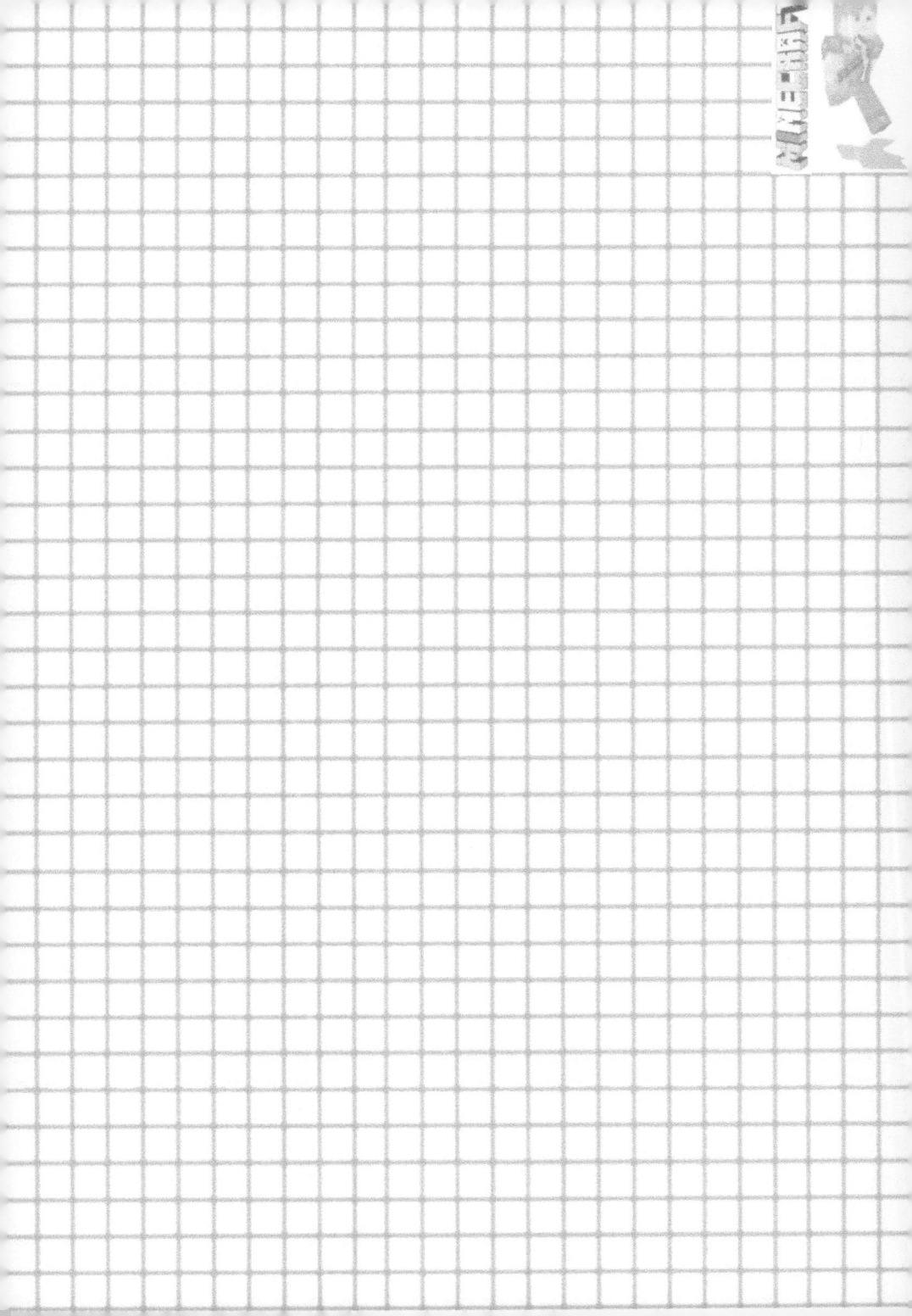

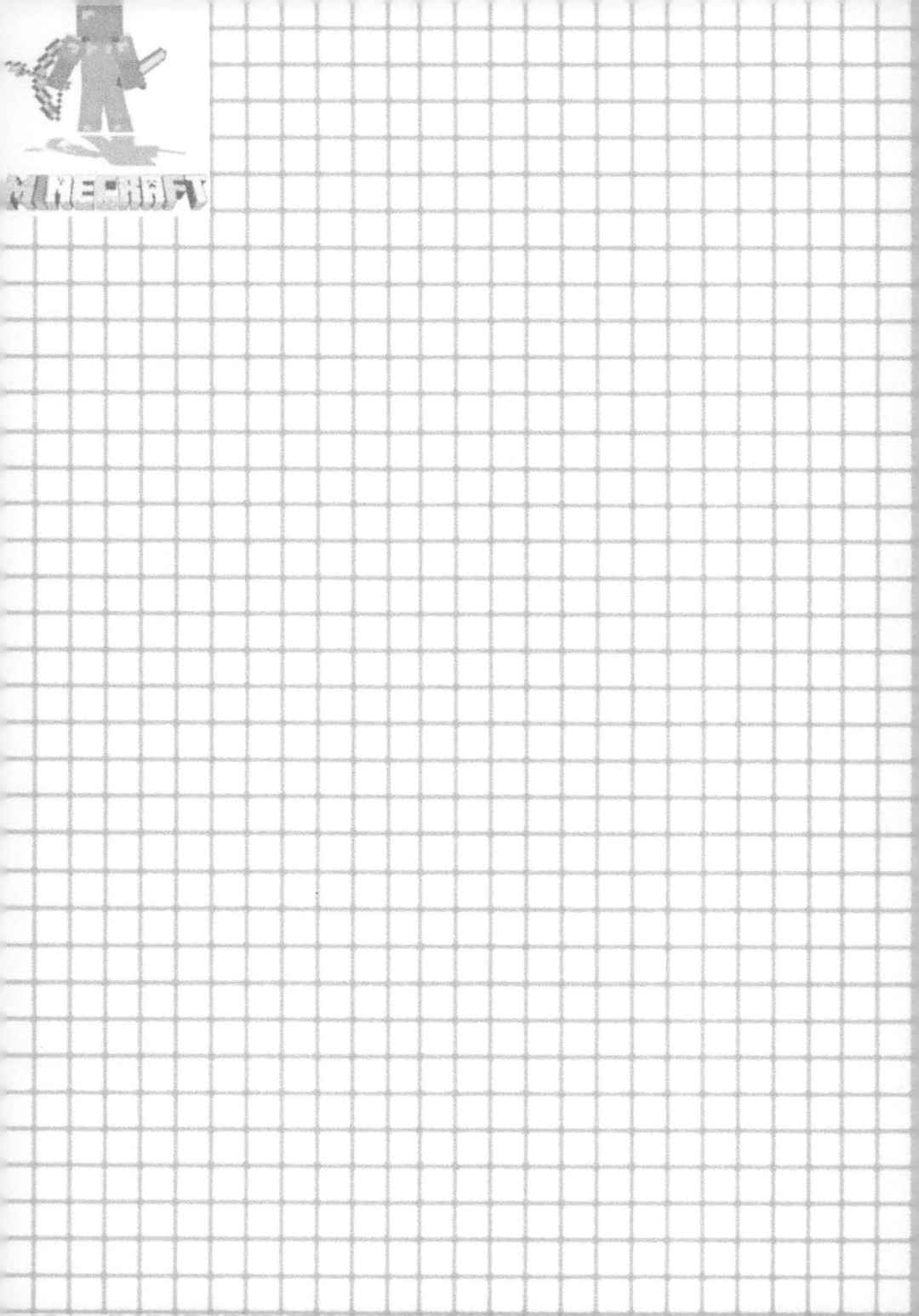

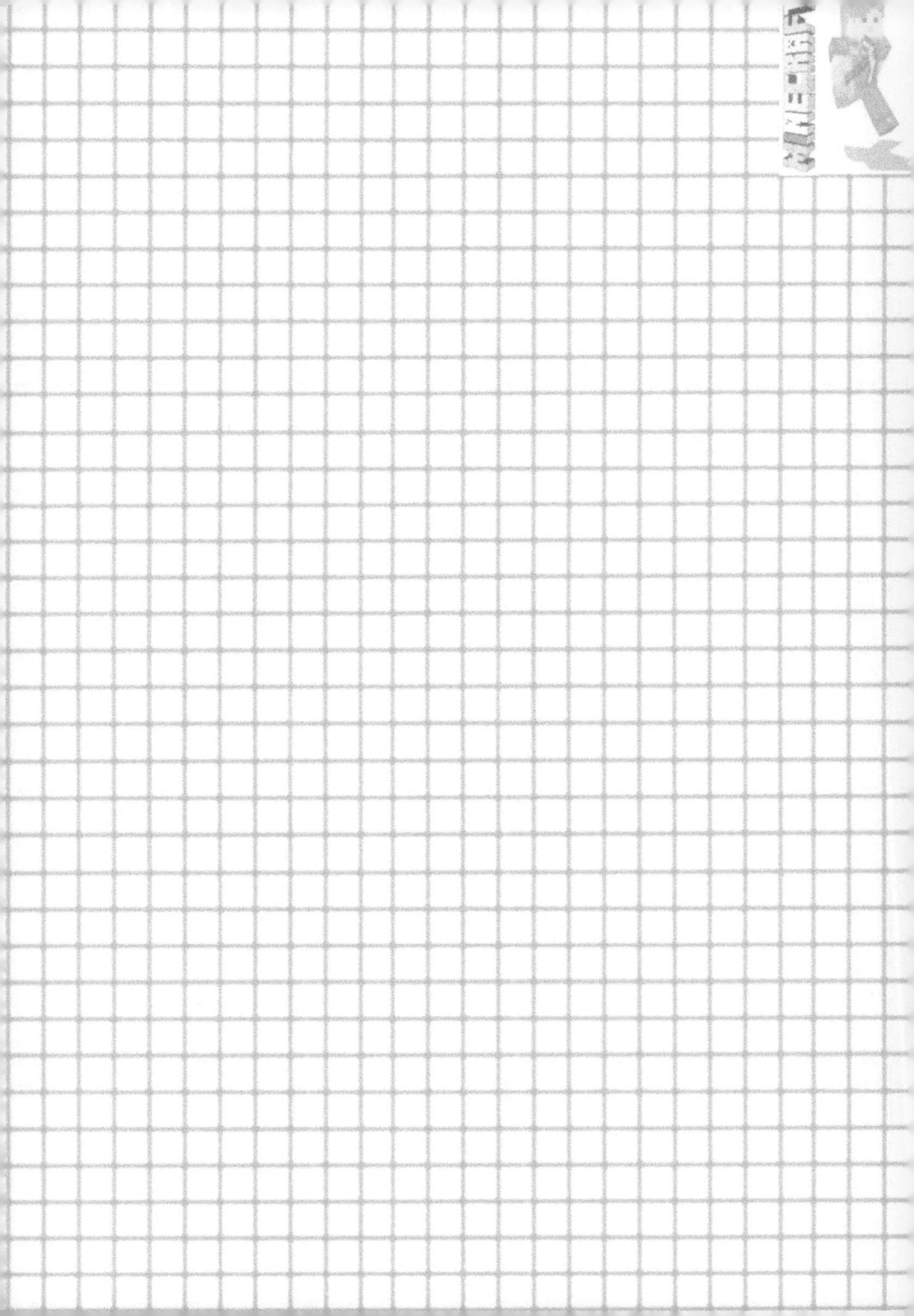

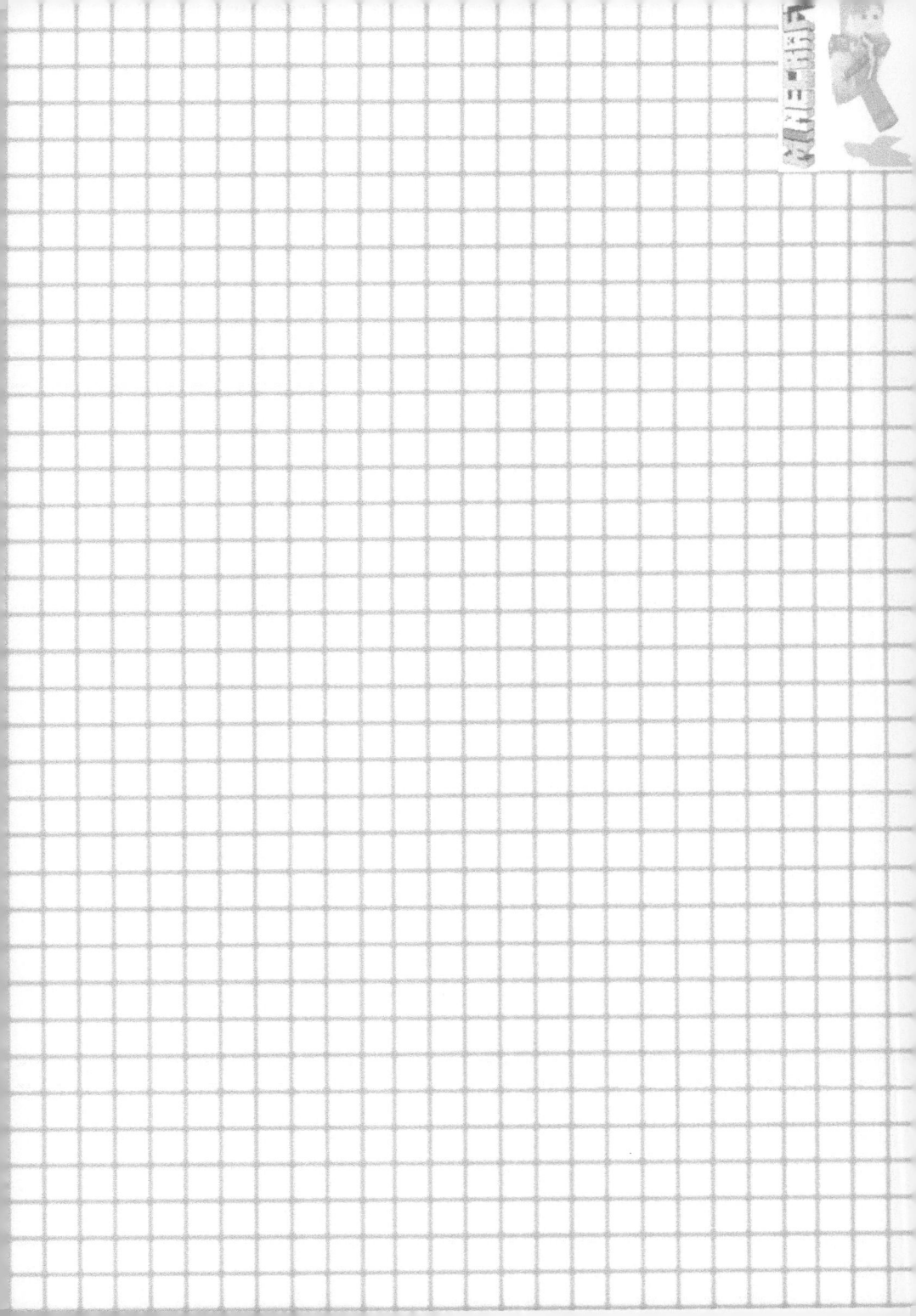

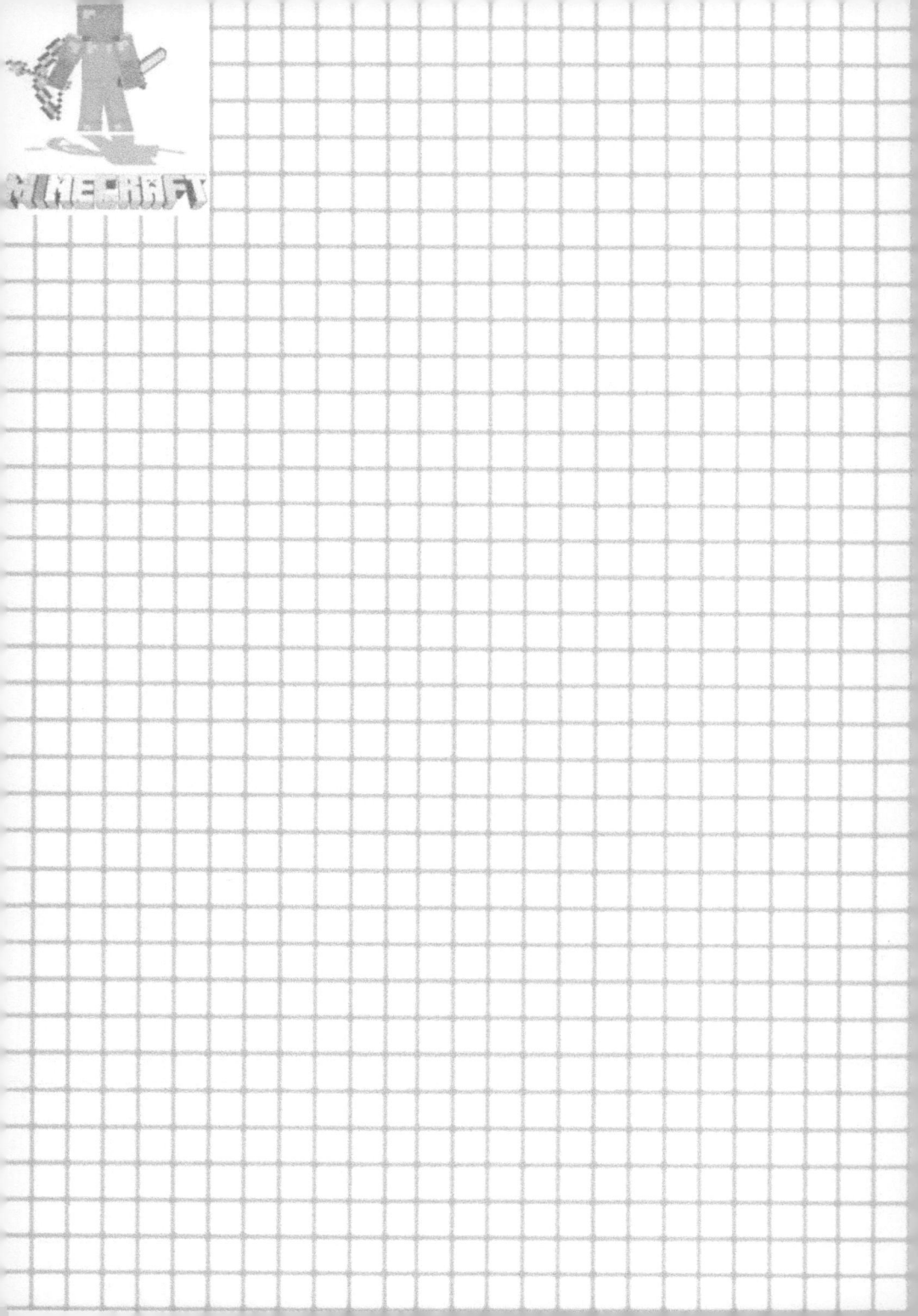

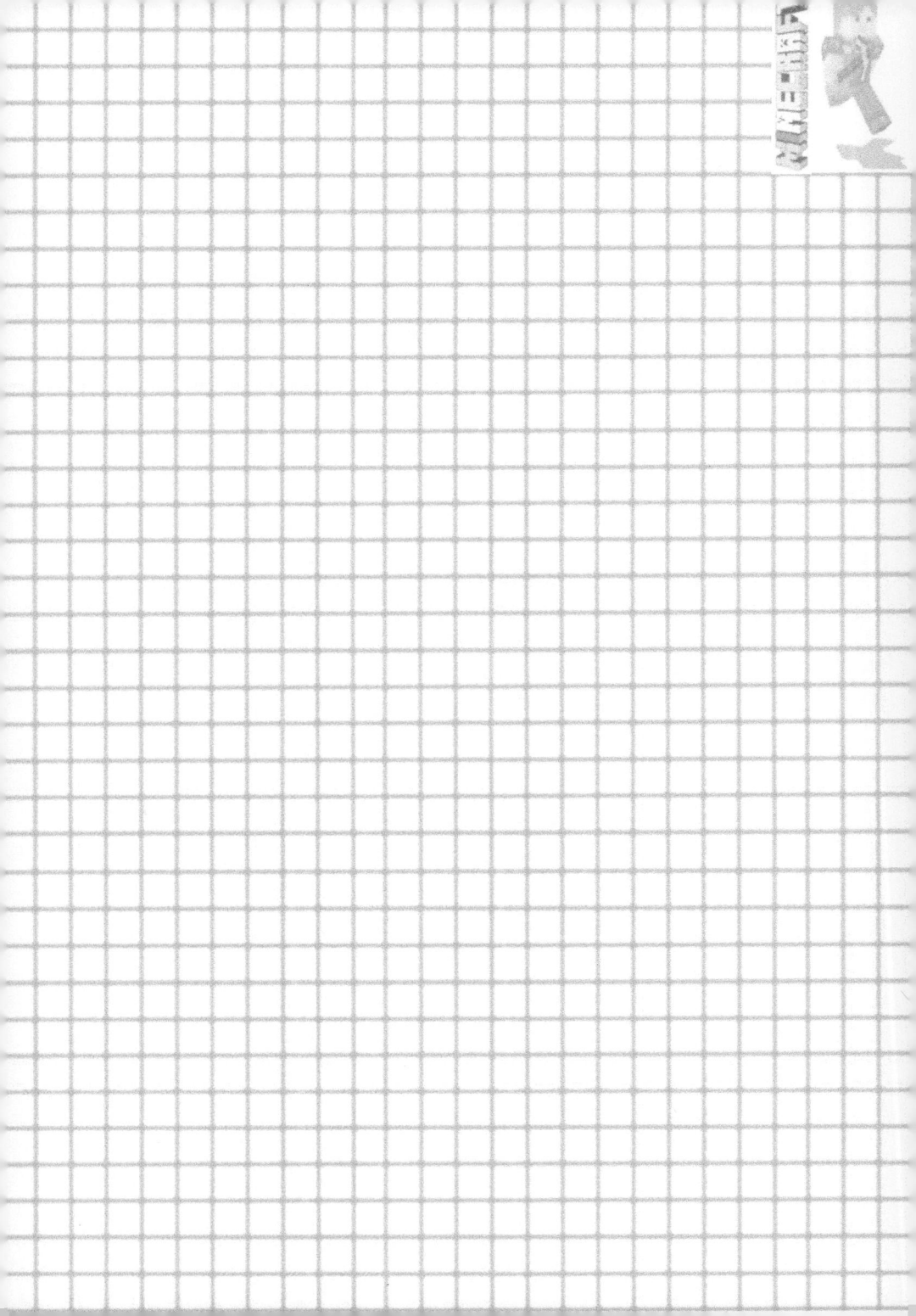

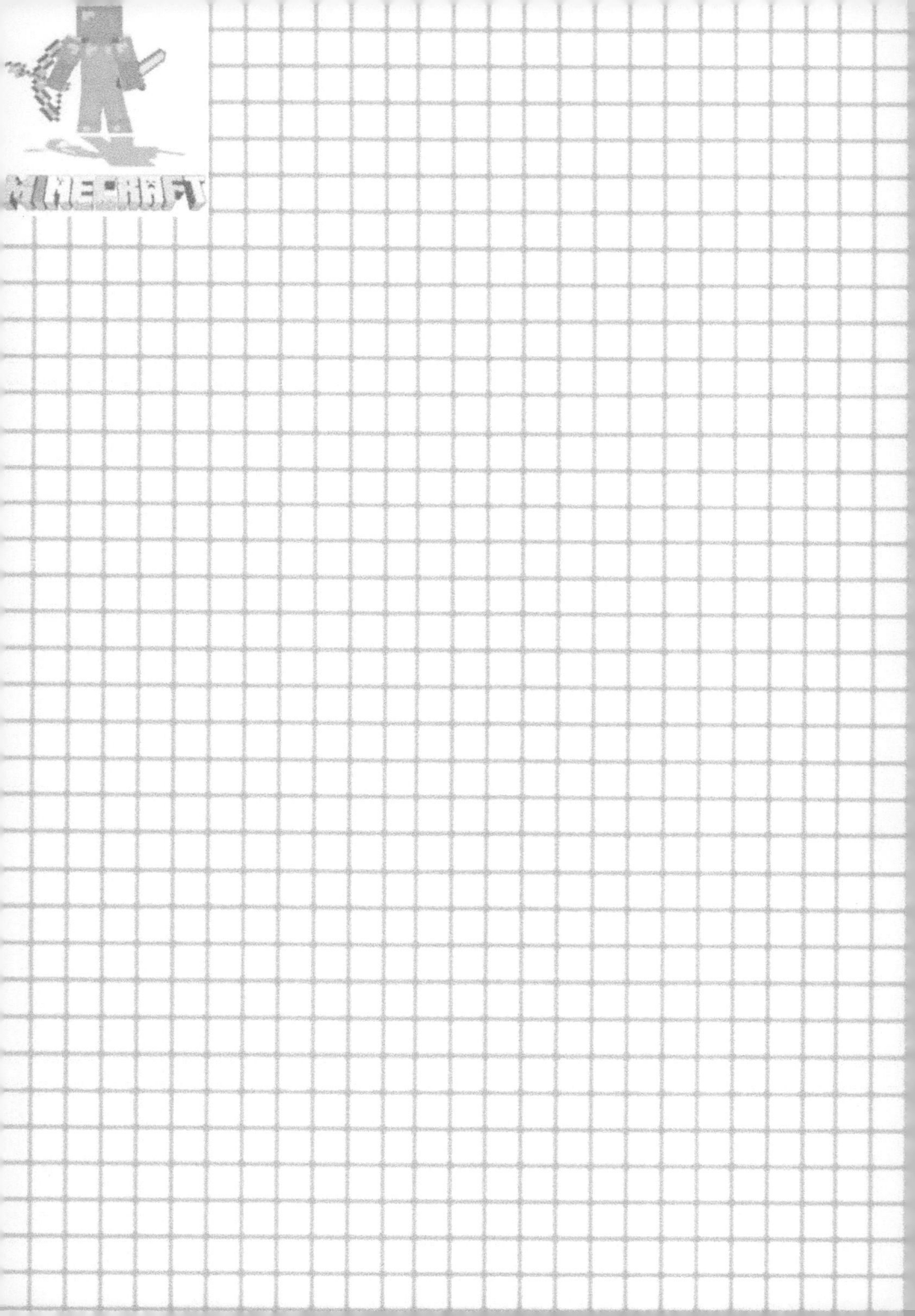

Weitere Bücher der FUNCRAFT Reihe:

Titel	Alter	ISBN
Funcraft - Das beste inoffizielle Mathe Ausmalbuch für Minecraft Fans (6-10 Jahre)	6-10	9783743196919
Funcraft - Das inoffizielle Mathe Ausmalbuch: Minecraft Minis (Cover Hase)	6-10	9783734781452
Funcraft - Das inoffizielle Mathe Ausmalbuch: Minecraft Minis (Cover Zombie)	6-10	9783743163744
Funcraft - Das inoffizielle Mathe Ausmalbuch: Minecraft Minis (Cover Dragon)	6-10	9783743182417
Funcraft - Das inoffizielle Mathe Ausmalbuch: Superhelden im Minecraft Skin (Cover Batman)	6-10	9783743192904
Funcraft - Das inoffizielle Mathe Ausmalbuch: Superhelden im Minecraft Skin (Cover Superman)	6-10	9783743192836
Funcraft - Das inoffizielle Witzebuch für Minecraft Fans	8-14	9783743192539
Funcraft - Noch mehr inoffizielle Witze für Minecraft Fans	8-14	9783743192607
Funcraft - Die besten inoffiziellen Witze für Minecraft Fans	8-14	9783743193192
Funcraft - Die lustigsten inoffiziellen Witze für Minecraft Fans	8-14	9783743195240
Funcraft - Das inoffizielle Rätselbuch für Minecraft Fans	8-14	9783743195387
Funcraft - Noch mehr inoffizielle Rätsel für Minecraft Fans	8-14	9783743195400
Funcraft - Das inoffizielle Offline Spielebuch für Minecraft Fans	8-14	9783743195424
Funcraft - Das inoffizielle Quizbuch für Minecraft Fans	8-14	9783741291203
Funcraft - Noch mehr inoffizielle Quizfragen für Minecraft Fans	8-14	9783739235592
Funcraft - Das inoffizielle Rekordebuch für Minecraft Fans	8-14	9783743165502
Funcraft - Das inoffizielle Hausaufgabenbuch für Minecraft Fans	8-14	9783743177666
Funcraft - Aufstand in Germanien (Ein Minecraft inspirierter Roman)	12-99	9783743196858
Funcraft - Eiszeitjäger: Auf der Fährte des Löwen (Ein Minecraft inspirierter Roman)	12-99	9783743196865
Funcraft - Das beste inoffizielle Notizbuch (liniert) für Minecraft Fans	6-99	9783743196872
Funcraft - Das inoffizielle Notizbuch (kariert) für Minecraft Fans	6-99	9783743196889
Funcraft - Frohes Neues Jahr an alle Minecraft Fans! (inoffizielles Notizbuch) - Das	6-99	9783743196896
Funcraft - Fröhliche Weihnachten an alle Minecraft Fans! (Inoffizielles Notizbuch)	6-99	9783743196902
Passwort Logbuch für Minecraft Fans	6-99	9783743163928
Pokefun - Das inoffizielle Witzebuch für Pokemon GO Fans	6-99	9783743109780
Pokefun - Das inoffizielle Quizbuch für Pokemon GO Fans	6-99	9783743109827
Pokefun - Das inoffizielle Notizbuch (Team Rot) für Pokemon GO Fans	6-99	9783743109841
Pokefun - Das inoffizielle Notizbuch (Team Gelb) für Pokemon GO Fans	6-99	9783743109858
Pokefun - Das inoffizielle Notizbuch (Team Blau) für Pokemon GO Fans	6-99	9783743109865
Pokefun - Das absolut inoffizielle Notizbuch für Pokemon GO Fans	6-99	9783743109834
Weltbester Radfahrer - Notizbuch	6-99	9783738610161
Weltbester Inline Skater - Notizbuch	6-99	9783738610178
Weltbester Skifahrer - Notizbuch	6-99	9783738610185
Weltbester Snowboarder - Notizbuch	6-99	9783738610192
Weltbester Sportler - Notizbuch	6-99	9783738610208
Weltbester Surfer - Notizbuch	6-99	9783738610215
Weltbester Taucher - Notizbuch	6-99	9783738610222
Weltbester Tennisspieler - Notizbuch	6-99	9783738610239
Weltbester Volleyballer - Notizbuch	6-99	9783738610246
Weltbester Wassersportler - Notizbuch	6-99	9783738610253

Von Theo von Taane gibt es weit mehr als 200 Witzebücher, Notizbücher, Romane, Spiele, Tools, Sportbücher und Kalender. Im Store einfach mal nach „Theo Taane" suchen.
Viel Spaß!